MW00510604

SWING TRADING

STRATEGIES AND GUIDE FOR BEGINNERS. DIFFERENT OPTIONS FOR RISK MANAGEMENT AND ANALYSIS. EASY RULES AND ROUTINES USED WHEN INVESTING IN STOCKS OR FOREX WHICH LEAD TO DIVIDEND PROFITS.

Table of Contents

Introduction

Swing trading is a strategy used by traders to generate profit from the stock market over days or weeks. The strategy makes use of technical trading to identify the right opportunities for traders. It also uses fundamental analysis to determine patterns and trends in stock prices.

Traders use this technique to purchase and sell stocks whose prices have a high change potential in future. They make profit from the upward or downward trend of the market. Trades must be completed as fast as possible in order to realize the best profits from swing trading.

Swing trading entails holding trading positions over several trading sessions. However, this only goes on for a number of days, weeks or months. The strategy utilizes short term methods of trading and cannot be applied to long-term trades spanning more than a year. Some of the financial instruments traded using this strategy include commodities, indexes, cryptocurrencies, bonds and stocks.

Technical analysis helps swing traders to identify the kinds of stocks whose price might either increase or decrease in the near future. Traders always analyze the technical indicators available on the market to identify such price movements. This enables them to estimate the right time to purchase or sell positions. As a trader, you main focus should be capitalizing on the price changes, in this case known as swings. Small profits made over time often grow into significant results. For instance, a long-term trader can wait for 6 months to make a profit of %20 from one trade while a swing trader can earn a profit of 5% every week from several trades. In the long run, the swing trader makes a lot more than other traders.

When swing trading, you can make use of daily, weekly or monthly charts to identify the right entry and exit positions for each trade. You can use the strategy on volatile stocks as well as on average ones. Either way, you can still make profit from any slight changes in stock prices. The aim is always to capture some returns from anticipated price movement then moving on to another opportunity.

Swing trading is considered an active form of trading just like day trading. Opportunities are selected based on reward/ risk percentages. These percentages are derived from trading charts. Each chart provides information on two forms of swings – the swing low and the swing high. The swing low occurs when the price of a certain financial instruments assumes a downward trend. The swing high occurs when the price of the instrument assumes an upward trend.

The work of the swing trader is to monitor how the price changes from low to high. When the cost of an instrument starts to increase, the trader makes a purchase from the low price and waits for the price to hit a maximum high to open a sell position. The standard procedure used in swing trading is as follows:

1. You purchase or sell a financial instrument that is trending on the market

2. The cost of the instrument indicates a potential rise or decline based on the necessary technical analysis carried out

3. You sell or purchase the instrument after a few to several days depending on the direction assumed by the market prices

4. You the close the position and repeat the same process using different positions and financial instruments.

The outcome of each swing trade is determined by how the market changes. Some predictions may not be as accurate as indicated by technical analysis tools. That is why you must be flexible when it comes to the outcome of each trade since you can make more or less than what you have anticipated.

There are several similarities between swing trading and day trading. The only difference is about the trading period. Day trading does not involve overnight holds, while swing trading does. A day trader must ensure closure of all positions before the trading day ends. A swing trading position can remain open for days, weeks and even months. The risk involved in swing trading is however larger than day trading because drastic changes to a stock price may occur during the night. Gaps may also occur due to some changes in financial news and this can result in tremendous gains, or losses.

Swing trading is often considered to be a combination of short and long-term trading strategies.

Chapter 1 Why Swing Trading Is Favorable For Beginner Traders

Swing trading is favorable for beginner traders for several reasons. Beginners are advised to start with swing trading when they join the markets because it does not need skills. Unlike other types of trading where you stand to lose a lot by trading without proper skills, swing trading is relatively easy. Swing traders only need to have the capital and you are ready to go. Some people shy away from swing trader because of the risks involved. If you do not have tolerance when you lose, you will not succeed at anything in life. Fearlessness enables people to accomplish their dreams as timid people watch. If you have been, dreaming of entering the trade market, use swing trading and you will not be disappointed. It saves you money you could have used to learn how to trade.

Swing trading is favorable for beginners because it is not time-consuming, like other types of trade. Once you hold a position, you can focus on other things. On the contrary, other types of trade such require you to monitor the stock regularly. As a beginner, you will have a lot of time in your hands if you choose swing trading.

Who would not want extra time to do other things in life? We all wish we could have more time to sleep, spend time with families or focus on personal growth. Swing trading gives you just that by eliminating the hassle of trading.

Another reason why swing trading is suitable for beginners is that it is stress-free. You can rest knowing that everything is in order. Many traders are restless because they are constantly worried about missing out on trading opportunities. What is worse is that when they make profits, they still need to monitor the market in search of stocks to invest in. It is a never-ending struggling that affects other areas of life. The stress you get from trading can harm your family in many ways than you think. Rather than spending time with your children, you spend the whole day trading. Things are worse when you lose because you are in a terrible mood and does not talk to people nicely. Different trading methods have drawbacks that should be considered before opting for them. A sure way to avoid stress as a beginner is to choose swing trading. Your mind is in a good place and relates nicely with people around you. Moreover, swing trading is favorable because it enables you to learn market trends, something you may not be able to do quickly with other types of trade. You are not in a rush when swing trading and this increase chances of making smart decisions. Adrenaline junkies love trading because it gets them high but this is not good if you want to win big in the markets. You need to be sober to evaluate stocks with clarity. Swing trading is suitable because it takes less time, thereby eliminates the rush that comes with trading. You are able to think clearly and minimize trading risks.

Swing trading is favorable for beginners because it allows them to hold separate jobs. Any type of trading can drain your account seriously. If you do not have enough money or a separate account, you may just become the next beggar. Many traders have suffered heavy blows from the markets after investing all their resources on stocks. It is not bad to take a risk if you feel it worth a try. However, it is wrong to use all your savings when you have a family to support. While you gain more than you invest, there is also a possibility you could lose. What would happen if you traded with everything you have and end up empty-handed? Successful traders have mastered the art of trading and how to survive in the long run. They set up a separate savings account to help them during rough times. The savings also helps to recover from trading loss. Swing trading increases chances of saving by giving you time to focus on other ventures. It is not a whole day affair and many swing traders have day jobs. They are less likely to be affected when they lose in the stock market because they have a steady income. Moreover, their children will continue with school because they have a savings account. Thus, swing trading is suitable for beginners because of the perks it offers. It eliminates the worry of where to get money or tools to use. Give it a try today and save yourself from the trouble of dealing with uncertain market movements. Most people prefer swing trade because chances of getting strong reward ratio are higher than loss ratio. The best advice you can take as a beginner is to pay attention to the reward/loss ratio. There is no point in buying stocks at a high and selling low. This is a waste of time and resources. Take time to study different stocks to gauge profitability. Another reason why people incur losses day and night is because of putting high leverages they cannot afford. Be careful with the decisions you make because they not only affect your trades but also your life. If it crumbles, other aspects of you are affected. When you fail, everyone who depends on you fails. Therefore, swing trading is favorable for beginners because you stand to gain more than lose. You also learn a lot of information from the stock market, which is useful in future, trades. It is not a must to choose other trading strategies once you stay long in the market. You can improve your skills and continue as a swing trader. It is better to continue with a strategy you know and have used before. In the end, you want to exit the market wiser than you entered, even if you incur losses. There is no better way to learn the stock market apart from swing trading.

Chapter 2 Swing Trading Guiding Principles

The routine of a Swing Trader

In order for a trader to be successful in their trade swinging, they need to spend a good amount of time on the markets analyzing and finding the loopholes. The first thing they need to do is begin their day slightly Earlier than the opening time of the markets, that is before the opening bell, which is rung at 6 am EST. This will help them get a general overview of what is expected and the things that should go into their watch list of the day, the potential trades they can cash in and the existing positions of the different trading instruments.

1) Market Overview

The second step is to look at the latest news across the world, that is both economically and politically to see what role these fundamental factors are likely to play on during the days trading time. This is because according to the fundamental analysts, if there a negative change in the political or economic structure of a certain nation or region, the odds of the currency of the affected areas going low are very high and the traders would like to have a step ahead in this so they can sell off and cut down on their losses. The trader can catch up on this news using either reliable websites such as a Market watch or watching television cable networks such as CNBC. While doing this, the trader should pay attention to three things; in particular, they include:

1. The market sentiment- this is the general feel of the market pattern that could either be bearish or bullish, it also involves looking out for the inflation fluctuations in the national currency and reading the economic reports that may have been released.

2. Sector sentiment- this is the general feel of the different economic sectors that make up an economy, such as the manufacturing sector, the agricultural sector etcetera. The general sectoral composition of an economy will tell the trader what the best move to make on a currency is. For instance, if the manufacturing sector of an economy is growing, the likelihood of the currency being strong is greater than the economy which is majorly focused on the agricultural sector

3. Current portfolio contents- the trading instruments in the current portfolio of a market are vital to any swing trader since they get to know what is hot on the market and vice versa. The news that is put forth on either futures or options, earnings, and regulations will come in handy when the trader has to make a decision.

Potential Trades

After a swing trader has conducted their market overview research and armed with the findings from this analysis, they are now set to scan for the potential trades they can engage in during the day. Normally, a swing trader will use the fundamental analysis to scan for the right entry positions before they apply their own technical analysis to get the perfect exit points. The three main methods swing traders utilize in getting the right fundamental catalysts for their entry points to include:

Special Opportunities

These are moments such as initial public offerings, mergers, acquisitions, and suspensions, takeovers and buyouts, bankruptcy announcements, insider buying, and restructuring, among other things. In such moments the swing trader will most likely do the opposite of what the trend is, they will buy when the trend is selling and sell when the trend is buying.

Sector Plays

This is similar to what the trade did in the market overview; they pay attention to certain sectors and hop on to the train as it embarks on its journey. Whenever a sign of a retracement appears the swing traders will alight the train since all they needed to do was ride the trend when it was perfect for them.

Chart Breaks

By analyzing the charts, swing traders will always note the different trading instruments that will be close to a resistance or support level. They will utilize patterns such as;

·   *Symmetrical Triangle patterns*
This is a continuation pattern that has at least two higher highs and lows and two lower lows.

The logic behind the symmetrical triangle pattern

Buyers will push the price in different directions as the sellers. The buyers will keep pushing the price up, making higher, and the sellers will equally push the price low making lower highs. This kind of narrowing of the trading range usually means that the buyers and sellers are both losing interests in that price level, and they may feel as though the security or pair is overrated. This explains why the pattern starts wide and begins to narrow towards the end of the pattern. When the trading range begins to narrow when either the buyers or sellers were having a kind of war, it signals the possibility of a big sharp move in either direction depending on who caves first among the buyers and sellers breaking the pattern. The narrowing also means there re low volumes of orders in the market at that specific level, since, the buyer considers the price level unattractive for them to purchase and the seller feels the price is not that attractive for him to sell either. However, when the price breaks out of this small range, it will move fast in one direction , all we can do as traders is wait prepared for the pattern to break in our predetermined direction of trade and with a stop order in the other direction because we must prepare for the worst even as we hope for the best.

· *Ascending Triangle Pattern*

This is a bullish continuation pattern that must have at least two highs and two lows that can be connected with more than one trend lines. The atop most trend line will have to be horizontal while the lower trend line has to be diagonal.

The logic behind ascending triangle patterns

The logic behind this continuation pattern is pretty obvious, and I am sure you can already tell what it is. If you thought that the sellers are not going down without a fight and the buyers are still breathing down their necks persistently, then you are right. The buyers will push the price higher making higher lows while the sellers insist on keeping the prices low at the level where the horizontal trend line is. Unfortunately, or fortunately, depending on what your predetermined direction is, the sellers will cave in and admit defeat and stop entering sell orders at the horizontal line since the buyers will counteract that move and push the price back up to the levels where they sold and triggered their stop losses. With this outnumbering of the sellers, the buyers will be in control of the market. After this spiff, the pattern will break, and the trend will resume the trend that had been established by the previous impulsive move.

· *Descending triangle pattern*
This is a continuation pattern that is literally the opposite of the ascending triangle pattern. It is a bearish continuation pattern which means that the trend is down

and the price will have to stop for a short period of time in order to consolidate, and this type of move forms a descending triangle pattern before the trend resumes going further down.

The logic behind Descending Triangle Patterns

This logic behind this particular pattern mirrors the one that is behind ascending triangle patterns. In this case, though the sellers are in large numbers and the trend is moving down. The buyers will hold their forte and keep it down at the horizontal trend line. Although this will only last a short period of time before the sellers, who are in the majority, win and break the pattern leading to a resumption of the trend downwards.

· *Price Channel*

This is a continuation pattern that is made up of two parallel trend lines, that is one above and the other below the price that takes the shape of a channel. This is a continuation pattern that is applicable in both the bullish and bearish markets. The distinction between these two markets is the direction the sloping will occur in. If the channel slopes upwards then his is considered a bullish continuation pattern and vice versa if the channel is sloping downward then we can consider this the bearish continuation pattern. Like the rest of the patterns, the trend lines have to be drawn while connecting at least two highs and two lows.

The logic behind Price channel continuation pattern

When the trend is up:

This means the buyers are in control in this case and the price will stop in order for it to consolidate when they eventually decide to take some of the profits out of the market, but in that specific moment, the sellers will be out of sight. The sellers are weak in this case and lack the strength to correct the trend or even make a minute move against the trend direction. Therefore, the price will just trickle on upwards, slowly forming a channel before the buyers eventually resume the strong trend by breaking the already slow-moving pattern and taking the movement further higher. This is the bullish price channel continuation pattern.

When the trend is down:

The vice versa of what happens in the bullish price channel continuation pattern will occur here since it is a bearish type of continuation pattern when the trend is moving down. In this case, it means the sellers are in control and the price will stop in order for it to consolidate when they eventually decide to take some of the profits out of the market but in that specific moment, the buyers will be out of sight. The buyers who are weak in this case will equally lack the strength to correct the trend or even make a minute move against the trend direction, therefore, the price will just trickle on downwards slowly forming a channel before the sellers eventually resume the strong trend by breaking the already slow-moving pattern and taking the movement further lower.

Creating a Watch List

Swing traders should now create a watch list after the analysis, on the different currencies they would like to keep an eye on. It is advisable for the list to have columns that show the target prices, the entry prices, and the stop-loss prices of each trading instrument.

Look at the Existing Positions

The traders must look at the positions that they are in at this pre-market hour before the opening bell sounds. With the fundamental analysis report at the back of their minds, they need to pay attention to the changes that are likely to be influenced, and if they stand to gain or lose their current positions. This is important because it always guides the trader on whether they should adjust either their stop-loss signals or their take-profit positions in order to adjust to the recent changes.

1) Market Hours

Once the opening bell sounds, the swing traders will look at who is buying and who is selling. They focus on the trend and plan their entry and exit using different analysis as discussed below.

2) Flag pattern trade example.

Let us assume the last impulsive move on the four-hour chart was down, when we check the thirty-minute chart we will have to wait for a continuation pattern to form. After it forms, we will wait for the price to break in the direction of the impulsive move on the four-hour chart. In this case, when the move was down, we are going to be seeking to sell, so we need the flag to break on the downside. Break-in this case means zooming out of the 30 minute chart and waiting for a thirty-minute candle to form and close outside below the flag pattern after this candle has closed out, zoom out of the thirty minutes chart and wait of the price to go back up to the red lower trend line and retest it (get close to it.) this will now be a Resistance line. When a pattern breaks and price comes back shortly to retest the line, this is what forms a resistance line. We should enter the sell stop order at the level where the price started to rise back up and retest the lower trend line of the flag. The Stop loss is placed where the retest of the trend line took place.

How to Manage the Stop Loss level

In the example above, when the price begins to move away from the flag pattern, it will form small lower highs! We should trail our stop loss levels manually to just above these lower highs.

There are two ways to enter the trade; the first one is the method discussed above where we wait for the retest of the pattern and the second one is to enter when a thirty-minute candle body is completely outside the pattern if the retest did not happen right after the first candle that closed outside it. The reason is that at times the trend will be too strong and the retest may never happen as speculated before.

3) Descending triangle trade example

Let us assume there is a clear downtrend with the most recent impulsive move on the four-hour chart moving down. The pattern then breaks to the downside as we would like it to break but after the first thirty minutes candle that closes tight outside our pattern and there is no retest on the lower trend line. If there is no retest after the first candle that breaks the pattern, then we should enter at the close of the second candle that is considerably outside the pattern. We should not wait for the retest as it did not happen after the first candle chances are it will not happen now either, we should place the stop loss above the last minor lower high that is inside the pattern. After that, we shall manually trail the stop-loss order as we did in the previous example where we entered the order after the patterns reset

4) Ascending triangle trade example

Let us assume there is a clear uptrend with the most recent impulsive move on the four-hour chart moving up, but there is no retest after the first candle that closes above the pattern. We will have to enter the trade at the close of the second candle, which should be completely out of the pattern. It is imperative to do this and make some pips instead of sitting around waiting on a retest that may very much not appear.

5) Rectangle pattern trade example

After the broken candle which closes outside the pattern, the retest of the resistance lines is put into play. We should enter the market when the price comes back down at the close of the breakout candle and set the stop loss in the places where the retest finished, and the prices started going down and away from the pattern and trend.

Exits

One of the exit strategies we have touched on is the stop-loss method where you can trail it manually to points just above the lower highs on the thirty-minute chart when selling or just below the higher knows if you are the buyer. These are considered the logical turning points in the market. They are the least likely levels that the price will touch whenever there is a strong direction, and this makes them a perfect spot to hang the stop loss.

The second way to exit the trade earlier than this moment which involves the wedge continuation pattern. We agreed that the wedge pattern could be either a continuation or a reversal pattern, and this depends on the location that the wedge is in. Just a reminder, if the wedge pattern forms at the correction phase of a huge trend on the four-hour chart and it slopes against the trend, then this is a continuation pattern, and we can use it to enter trades. The wedge pattern can also emerge in the impulsive moves of the trend, indicating that the trend is about to come to a stop. The slope of the pattern, in this case, should be in line with the trend. The moment you spot this pattern emerging, you should keep an eye out for the breaking of the trend, which is the confirmation of the end of the said trend.

The main approach for trade exists still remains the manual trailing of stop-loss either below or above the logical points. However, if you see a wedge that will break to the downside if the last impulsive move is an uptrend or breaks to the upside if the last impulsive move on the four hour chart is a downside then you as the trader should exit when the pattern breaks and a 30 minute candle forms outside to signify the end of the trend. This is actually a better exit level since you do not need to wait for the price rise till it gets to the last high or go down to the last low so that your stop loss level is hit and the order materializes eating away at a small part of your profits.

· *Head and Shoulders pattern*
This is a trend formation that shows a reversal and formed by a certain peak which is considered a shoulder and then followed by a taller peak which is ahead, and a shorter peak (shoulder) follows suit and so on so forth. When the lowest points of two troughs are connected by

a line, this line is called the neckline. The neckline can either slope down or upwards. When the line slopes down, it indicates a more reliable signal. A target can be calculated by measuring the distance from the neckline to the topmost point of the head in the chart. This difference is a representation of how far the price will move up after it goes past the neckline. It is also the same distance that the price will make once it falls below the neckline.

At the end of the day, traders should always remember that they should not adjust their positions to take on more risk. They should instead make adjustments to either lock in profits o to take in more profit taking levels.

6) After Hours Market

After trading doing the day, traders are required to do a performance evaluation after the closing time of the markets. The report should have a good and clear recording of the trades that have either won or lost during the day. These reports will be used for both monitoring the performance and evaluating it as well as in the case of tax compliance. After the evaluations, traders are required to record their closing positions of all the open trades while paying close attention to the announcements that have been made after hours in order to help them in their pre-market analysis the following day.

The routine of a swing trader shows that one needs to plan diligently and prepare properly since the pre-market hours help them identify the potential trades and market opportunities of the day, the market hours are then spent enacting the conclusions that were drawn in the morning on the different positions and the after-hours are for evaluating the day's work and ensuring that the same thing that was written down in theory still happened practically.

How to Scan for Swinging Trade

This involves the use of a market radar which literally shows the trader where their counterparts are and what their moves are. The market radars can be easily incorporated in the different market scanners that are available all over the internet. We will discuss five different market radars that the trader can incorporate into their market scanners so that they do not miss out on any trading opportunity.

1. ADX Trend Scan

This is a swinging trading strategy that is also known as finding the Holy Grail. It involves looking for retracements within any trend that is considered perfect and healthy. For the long traders, they are required to use a 30 period ADX which should be indicating that it is above 30 and still going higher, their retracement levels should be a 20 simple moving average that the price should hit, once the price hits here, the traders should now order at the topmost point of the bar that is in contact with the 20 periods simple moving average. The short-term traders should use a 14-period ADX that is also above thirty and keeps on climbing higher; their retracement level should also be at the 20-period simple moving average, however, when the bar touches the simple moving average, the trader should sell at the lowest point that is in contact.

2. ADX Range Trades Galore

This is the indicator that looks around at the sideways moving markets for different trade setups such as the Gimmee Bar which is a market entry trading strategy that has the trader looking for a reversal pattern that is moving from the highest point of a trading range or the vice versa. In the long trader's point of view, the Gimmee bar trading strategy has prices which are considered to be going down and losing in a trading range. These prices should further touch the lower Bollinger band and form another bar that will always end at a higher position than the initial start-up position. This bar is known as the Gimmee bar that the trader should then consider buying just slightly above. The short-term traders, on the other hand, will deal with prices that will be seen as rising and going up in a trading range and touching the higher Bollinger band. They should then form another bar that will always end at a point that is considerably lower than the position where it opened, this bar known as the Gimmee bar is the spot that indicates where traders should sell at. The spot should be just slightly below this bar. However, should this bar cross and overlap the Moving average, or record a much wider range than the other Bollinger bands and bars, or alternatively open and go further than the range of the bars, the trader is advised to let go and not trade with the Gimmee bars. Whenever the ADX increases, it shows that the trend is supposedly getting stronger while the slight motion of the ADX in a downward trend will indicate the trading ranges required for analysis.

3. Hull Moving Average

While most of the traders are only aware of two moving averages, the Hull moving average is considered an exotic MA that helps the traders scan the waves in the markets and charts. Once the Hull Moving Average has been drawn on a chart, it is most likely to be way smoother than the actual market price while still flowing with the different ups and downs in the markets that form waves. The trader is advised to track down these turning points and use them to analyze the market waves and see the reversals and continuations likely to come up. If the slope of the Hull Moving Average is positive, then the trend that is being implied is the bull swing which is just stating and the vice versa, if the slope is negative then the trend that has begun is known as the bear swing.

4. Extreme Volume

If the volume is high, the odds of the trends ending or new trending breaking out are very high. Large trading volumes always lead to the appearance of exhaustion gaps, which usually appear immediately after the trend has come to a stop. It is caused by an increase of the last-minute buyers who get into a bullish market at the end of the trend right before the reversal commences. The gap will always close after about five different bars. Therefore, this is the windfall that the swing traders should look for if they want to make the move that they need to cash in their profits.

5. Impulse system scan

The first rule of trading usually does not trade against the trend; the other rule of swing trading does not trade against the impulse system momentum. That is considered a suicidal move that will most likely land you in a series of bad trades that will make you lose a lot. The impulse system scan uses a combination of two indicators that is the Moving Average Convergence Divergence and the Exponential Moving Average to scan the market and figure out its momentum. According to researchers, when these two indicators cross, that is the implication of an impulsive move that is often found in the trading psychology of human beings. The higher the time frame that the trader employs in this specific moment, the better and improve their trading set up will be. A long-term trader who is using a 13 period should have the exponential moving average in a rising pattern and the (12,26,9) Moving Average Convergence Divergence indicator forming a histogram that seems to be going higher too. These positions should encourage the trader should get into the market. The short-term trader should use the same indicators as well, but the difference is the indicators should show a position that is going lower. This is a colored indicator which has the blue color scheme code that indicates the disagreeing session of both indicators, the green color scheme should show a positive impulse which is ideal for long term traders and the red color scheme indicates the negative impulse systems which means the prices are falling which is perfect for short term traders.

How to buy low and sell high

When it comes to trading, you will realize that it does not just understand that basics like you would go to the market get your apple. The first thing that you will need is a frame of reference. You should have a technique on a chart where help you understand that this is relatively a low priced hence the possible time to enter the trade. You will need two methods if you want to make it trade entry.

You will need support and a resistant chart to help you know when it is time to enter the market. With this, you will look back historically to know where there is a low price. You, therefore, work on the probability of knowing where the resistance and supports are. You also need a confirmation of the market before you buy. You should not just buy because the prices are low. Look for a sign of strength where the candle has a bullish close. You will find that the buyers are stepping in here and there is a good chance that the market could hit higher.

When you want to sell, you should be looking for high prices; thus, you need to know the high price area from your chart. You also need to note the high cost that you are targeting. You will note that sometimes the swing partner will get shorter and shorter. You will, therefore, use the partner. You will ask yourself on what level of the chart is there an opposing pressure that is coming in right that will go against my trade. You know that sellers come in at swing highs, resistance or coming in at a previous support time resistance. If you want to make it, then you need to sell on a low swing level as you will be able to make more at that point. It is a minor support period, and support may become resistant. That is the best place to exit the trade on one swing of the market. Pay attention to the first level that swings high and take your partial profits. Sellers may be looking for areas of reasonable prices since there is a good chance that the market could reverse from there.

Chapter 3 Platforms And Tools For Trading

To be a successful trader, you will need access to reliable resources. The good news is that there are plenty of excellent resources all across the web. These resources include educational materials, online brokers, real-time securities markets data, and super-fast computer networks.

Sometimes you may not have access to all the resources necessary and you may have to choose between what is essential and what you can afford. A little research goes a long way in helping you make crucial decisions about your trades. It is advisable to know more about the kind of resources available to you. These resources are ideal for swing traders.

Swing Trading Tools

Traders are always searching for the best trading systems and ways they can develop these systems to suit their trading styles. Fortunately, there is a process that any trader can use in order to discover their preferred trading mode and system.

Identifying Best Strategies for Profitability

There are plenty of small but crucial things you can do as a swing trader to improve your success. For instance, you could begin by identifying the location of the swing low and swing high positions on a particular chart. If you are able to note the swings accurately, then you will be able to place accurate trades which will increase your profitability greatly.

Swing Highs and Swing Lows

Swing highs and swing lows are also referred to as SHSL. This refers to the price action where multiple bars and candlesticks are joined together so that they are viewed as a single move in a given direction. The movement is generally known as a leg. Sometimes it is also known as swing or a move. This is where the term swing originates from.

The swing represents a single part of the price action in a particular direction. This swing is always closely countered by a swing in the opposite direction. Sometimes this movement is sideways rather than back and forth. As it is, price moves back and forth in the market. In other words, it swings back and forth and hence the term swing. The highest point of a swing is the swing high while the lowest point is known as the swing low.

How to Identify Swings

The market is constantly in motion. A swing occurs when there are two consecutive lower highs and lower lows or when there are two consecutive higher lows and higher highs. Remember that swings appear in all manner of shapes and sizes. However, the rule on how to identify them is very simple. Simply look for consecutive higher highs and higher lows or consecutive lower highs and lower lows.

Swings are bullish if the general movement is upwards and bearish if the general movement is downwards. Sometimes a new low will appear when the trend is upwards. At other times a new high will appear when the general trend is headed downwards. When this happens, you should not be worried or concerned as these are considered false swings. Unless there are consecutive highs or lows, then ignore everything else.

Use Swings to Increase Profitability

We have learned how to identify swings in the market. Now we need to apply this knowledge in order to be profitable. The first step is to place your stop-loss points.

This should be slightly above the higher high for a bearish situation and below the lowest low in a bullish situation.

Also, the correct and accurate swing highs and swing lows provide an opportunity to draw Fibonacci extensions. These lines will enable you to identify target areas of high probability. As such, it becomes possible to place our take profit and stop-loss points on our charts. Remember Livermore? The gentleman said to be one of the most successful traders ever? Back in 19 29, he managed to make about $100 million. In today's terms, this is equivalent to almost $1.4 billion. That is a lot of money even for an experienced trader.

If you learn about the best trading systems, then you too can make plenty of money in today's prevailing marketing rates. You could always trade with the market trend or against it. Remember that it is always advisable to follow the trend rather than the opposite. Only oppose the trend if you are an experienced swing trader and know exactly what you are doing. Key will be identifying the best entry points into a trade and the best places to collect profits as well as exit trades.

Before you begin your swing, trading ventures, ensure that you come up with a tested plan that you can implement. Therefore, test your preferred systems and strategies and ensure that they are working as desired. This way, you will be able to prepare appropriately and trade successfully and profitably over time.

Swing traders are always searching for conditions in the markets where stock prices are looking to swing either downwards or possibly upwards. There are numerous technical indicators that are available to enhance your trades. Indicators used in swing trading are basically essential in identifying trends in the market between certain trading periods.

These trading periods that range anywhere from 3 to 15 are then analyzed using our technical indicators in order to determine the presence or otherwise of resistance and support levels. If these have actually materialized and are clearly visible, then we can proceed to make other determinations.

At this stage, you will also need to determine whether any trend is bullish or bearish. You will also need to be on the lookout for a reversal because without one you will not be able to enter a trade. Reversals are also referred to as countertrends or pullbacks. As soon as we can clearly point out the reversal, then we can easily identify the appropriate entry point.

The entry point should be the point where the pullback is just about to come to an end and the trend is about to pick up again. Being able to determine these points is really crucial. This same approach is the very same one used by Jesse Livermore to earn his wealth.

Benefits

Swing trading offers some of the best risks to reward opportunities compared to other trading strategies. This means that for a smaller amount, you will stand to win a much larger profit. Trading is a risky venture but swing trading has a better payoff compared to others. As such, you stand to make more money at reduced risks compared to traders using different trading styles like day traders or position traders.

Another benefit is that a lot of intraday noise will be eliminated using this approach. Smart money traders are always on the lookout for big swings and this is what you will also be doing. This approach is less stressful and potentially more profitable compared to other strategies.

You will also have a lot of time in your hands compared to other traders. Day traders and others often spend hours each day glued to their screens. Their days are not just spent staring at the screen but their stress levels are extremely high. Constant stress will result in fast burn-out and emotional trading which are not good for long-term successful trading.

Best Indicators for Swing Traders

There are plenty of indicators that traders and investors use to enhance their trades. We shall review just a few of these and discover the best way of applying them to our trades in order to maximize profitability. It is crucial to understand that none of these indicators will make you profitable from the onset. Therefore, do not break your back trying to find the best or most profitable trade indicators. Instead, focus more on learning about a couple of extremely effective indicators as well as the strategies and methods used alongside them. Experts believe that trading strategies are more profitable when you apply the few indicators that you have mastered.

1. Moving Averages

Moving averages are among the most important trade indicators used by swing traders. They are defined as lines drawn across a chart and are determined based on previous prices. Moving averages are really simple to understand yet they are absolutely useful when it comes to trading the markets. They are extremely useful to all kinds of traders include swing traders, day, intra, and long-term investors.

You need to ensure that you have a number of moving averages plotted across your trading charts all with different time periods. For instance, you can have the 100-day moving average, the 50-day, and the 9-day MA. This way, you will obtain a much broader overview of the market and be able to identify much stronger reversals and trends.

How to use Moving Averages

Once you have plotted and drawn the moving averages on your charts, you can then use them for a number of purposes. The first is to identify the strength of a trend. Basically, what you need to do is to observe the lines and gauge their distance from the current stock price.

A trend is considered weak if the trend and the current price are far from the relative MA. The farther they are then the weaker the trend is. This makes it easier for traders to note any possible reversals and also identify exit and entry points. You should move averages together with additional indicators, for instance, the volume.

Moving averages can also be used to identify trend reversals. When you plot multiple moving averages, they are bound to cross. If they do, then this implies a couple of things. For instance, crossing MA lines indicate a trend reversal. If these cross after an uptrend, then it means that the trend is about to change direction and a bearish one is about to appear.

However, some trend reversals are never real so you have to be careful before calling out one. Many traders are often caught off guard by these false reversals. Therefore, confirm them before trading using other tools and methods. Even then, the moving average is a very vital indicator. They enable traders to get a true feel and understanding of the markets.

2. RSI – Relative Strength Index

Another crucial indicator that is commonly used by swing traders and other traders are the RSI or relative strength index. This index is also an indicator that evaluates the strength of the price of a security that you may be interested in. The figure indicated is relative and provides traders with a picture of how the stock is performing relative to the markets. You will need information regarding volatility and past performance. All traders, regardless of their trading styles, need this useful indicator. Using this relative evaluation tool gives you a figure that lies between 1 and 100.

Tips on RSI Use

The relative strength index is ideally used for identifying divergence. Divergence is used by traders to note trend reversals. We can say that divergence is a disagreement or difference between two points. There are bearish and bullish divergent signals. Very large and fast movements in the markets sometimes produce false signals. This is why it advisable to always use indicators together with other tools.

You can also use the RSI to identify oversold and overbought conditions. It is crucial that you are able to identify these conditions as you trade because you will easily identify corrections and reversals. Sometimes securities are overbought at the markets when this situation occurs, it means that there is a possible trend reversal and usually the emerging trend is bearish. This is often a market correction. Basically, when a security is oversold, it signals a correction or bullish trend reversal but when it's overbought, it introduces a bearish trend reversal.

The theory aspect of this condition requires a ratio of 70:30. This translates to 70% overvalued or over purchased and 30% undervalued or oversold. However, in some cases, you might be safer going with an 80/20 ratio just to prevent false breakouts.

3. Volume

When trading, the volume is a crucial indicator and constitutes a major part of any trading strategy. As a trader, you want to always target stocks with high volumes as these are considered liquid. How many traders, especially new ones, often disregard volume and look at other indicators instead.

While volume is great for liquidity purposes, it is also desirable for trend. A good trend should be supported by volume. A large part of any stock's volume should constitute part of any trend for it to be a true and reliable trend.

Most of the time traders will observe a trend based on price action. You need to also be on the lookout for new money which means additional players and volume. If you note significant volumes contributing to a trend, then you can be confident about your analysis. Even when it comes to a downtrend, there should be sufficient volumes visible for it to be considered trustworthy. A lack of volume simply means the stock has either been undervalued or overvalued.

4. Bollinger Bands Indicator

One of the most important indicators that you will need is the Bollinger band indicator. It is a technical indicator that performs two crucial purposes. The first is to identify sections of the market that are overbought and oversold. The other purpose is to check the market's volatility.

This indicator consists of 3 distinct moving averages. There is a central one which is an SMA or simple moving average and then there two on each side of the SMA. These are also moving averages but are plotted on either side of the central SMA about 2 standard deviations away.

Accumulation and Distribution Line

Another indicator that is widely used by swing traders is the accumulation/distribution line. This indicator is generally used to track the money flow within security. The money that flows into and out of stock provides useful information for your analysis.

The accumulation/distribution indicator compares very well with another indicator, the OBV, or the on-balance volume indicator. The difference, in this case, is that it considers the trading range as well as the closing price of a stock. The OBV only considers the trading range for a given period.

When the security closes out close to its high, then the accumulation/distribution indicator will add weight to the stock value compared to closing out close to the mid-point. Depending on your needs and sometimes the calculations, you may want to also use the OBV indicator.

You can use this indicator to confirm an upward trend. For instance, when it is trending upwards, you will observe buying interest because the security will close at a point that is higher than the mid-range. However, when it closes at a point that is lower than the mid-range, then the volume is indicated as negative and this indicates a declining trend.

While using this indicator, you will also want to be on the lookout for divergence. When the accumulation/distribution begins to decline while the price is going up, then you should be careful because this signals a possible reversal. On the other hand, if the trend starts to ascend while the price is falling, then this probably indicates a possible price rise in the near future. It is advisable to ensure that your internet and other connections are extremely fast especially when using these indicators as time is of the essence.

The Average Directional Index, ADX

Another tool or indicator that is widely used by swing traders is the average directional index, the ADX. This indicator is basically a trend indicator and its purpose is largely to check the momentum and strength of a trend. A trend is believed to have directional strength if the ADX value is equal to or higher than 40. The directional could be upward or downward based on the general price direction. However, when the ADX value is below 20, then we can say that there is no trend or there is one but it is weak and unreliable.

You will notice the ADX line on your charts as it is mainline and is often black in color. There are other lines that can be shown additionally. These lines are DI- and DI+ and in most cases are green and red in color respectively. You can use all the three lines to track both the momentum and the trend direction.

Aroon Technical Indicator

Another useful indicator that you can use is the Aroon indicator. This is a technical indicator designed to check if financial security is trending. It also checks to find out whether the security's price is achieving new lows or new highs over a given period of time.

You can also use this technical indicator to discover the onset of a new trend. It features two distinct lines which are the Aroon down line and the Aroon up line. A trend is noted when the Aaron up line traverses across the Aaron down line. To confirm the trend, then the Aaron up line will get to the 100-point mark and stay there.

The reverse holds water as well. When the Aroon down line cuts below the Aaron up line, then we can presume a downward trend. To confirm this, we should note the line getting close to the 100-point mark and staying there.

This popular trading tool comes with a calculator which you can use to determine the number of things. If the trend is bullish or bearish, then the calculator will let you know. The formulas used to determine this refer to the most recent highs and lows. When the Aroon values are high, then recent values were used and when they are low, the values used were less recent. Typical Aroon values vary between o and 100. Figures that are close to 0 indicate a weak trend while those closer to 100 indicate a strong trend.

The bullish and bearish Aroon indicators can be converted into one oscillator. This is done by making the bearish one range from 0 to -100 while the bullish one ranges from 100 to 0. The combined indicator will then oscillate between 100 and -100. 100 will indicate a strong trend, 0 means there is no trend while -100 implies a negative or downward trend.

This trading tool is pretty easy to use. What you need to is first obtain the necessary figures then plot these on the relevant chart. When you then plot these figures on the chart, watch out for the two key levels. These are 30 and 70. Anything above the 70-point mark means the trend is solid while anything below 30 implies a weak trend.

Trading Platforms

Trading platforms are the actual platforms or software programs that enable traders to place their trades and monitor their accounts. An electronic trading platform is a computer program of a website with a user interface where traders place financial trades.

As a swing trader, you will use this platform to enter, close, exit, and manage positions. This is often done via an intermediary such as your broker. Most traders use online platforms which are overseen and offered by brokerage firms. Brokers charge a fee when you use their platforms but sometimes, they offer discounts to traders who make a certain number of trades each month or those with funded accounts.

Basic Swing Trading Platforms

Trading platforms provide traders with the opportunity to place trades and monitor their accounts. There is a variety of platforms available to swing traders. They come with a number of different features. These include premium research functions, a news feed, charting tools, and even real-time price quotes. These additional features and tools enhance a trader's performance and make it easier to execute trades faster and accurately. Most platforms available today are designed for different financial instruments like Forex, stocks, futures, and options.

We basically have two different types of platforms. These are commercial platforms and prop platforms. Commercial platforms are mostly used by traders such as swing traders, retail investors, and day traders. They are largely easy to use and come with a myriad of features such as charts and a news feed.

We also have prop platforms. These are platforms that are customized for specific users such as institutional investors and large brokerage firms. Apparently, their needs are much different compared to those of small traders and retail investors. The prop platforms are designed to take into consideration the different needs of these special clients.

As a swing trader, you will most likely be using commercial platforms provided by different brokerage firms. Even then, there are some things that you need to be on the lookout before choosing one. For instance, what are the included features? How about costs and fees charged? Also, different traders will require different tools on their platforms. There are certain tools that are suitable for day and swing traders while others are more suitable for options and futures traders.

When selecting a platform, always watch out for the fees charged. As a small-scale, retail swing trader, you want to trade on one that charges low and affordable fees. However, sometimes there are certain trade-offs. For instance, some platforms charge low fees but they lack certain crucial features or provide poor services. Others may seem expensive but provide crucial features including research tools and excellent services. So, you will need to consider all these factors before eventually selecting a suitable trading platform.

There is yet another crucial point to keep in mind when selecting a trading platform. Some platforms are available only through specific brokers or intermediaries. Other platforms are universal and work with different brokerage platforms and intermediaries across the board. Traders also select trading platforms based on their own personal styles and preferences.

You should find out if there are any particular requirements or conditions that require to be fulfilled. For instance, some platforms require traders to maintain at least $25, oo0 in their trading accounts in the form of equity and possibly cash as well. In this instance, a trader may then receive approval for credit which is also known as margin.

Examples of Swing Trading Platforms

1. The Home Trading System

The home trading system is an algorithm and trading software designed to improve performance. Using this system, you can expect to make smarter, faster and better trading decisions. This particular platform comes with innovative features and a custom algorithm that combines seamlessly to provide a real-time fully integrated trading platform. You are bound to benefit from this platform and experience the benefits of seamless trading complete with all the features that you need.

The platform is completely compatible with some of the most dynamic and highly reliable charting tool. It is able to work with all kinds of markets from stocks to Forex and indices. The platform is compatible with a variety of bars such as range and momentum bars as well as tick charts.

The designers of this platform took great care to consider all the different kinds of traders. This is why this specific platform is suitable for day traders, swing traders, Forex traders, retail investors, and long-term traders. The Home Trading System constitutes a modular platform that consists of different core features. A lot of these features can easily be switched off and on depending on the situation or to suit a particular requirement.

One of the advantages of this platform is that it endeavors to make trading extremely simple. For instance, the algorithm automatically colors the candlesticks or bars a red or blue color in order to provide a clear view of the market conditions and trends. The system will continue following the trends and mark any major changes in a contrasting color. For instance, whenever there is a trigger bar, these will appear in a different color so that it is clear to you the trader that there is definite variation in the trend.

This color feature not only makes trading easy but also improves your trading psychology so that you can trade with very little worry. Other desirable parameters that are essential to your trades are also provided on the platform. For instance, you need accurate and reliable trading signals delivered at the right time. Fortunately, the Home Trading System is designed to provide these signals in a timely and accurate manner.

When there is a turning point in the momentum of stock in the markets, then this will be detected and a change of color will clearly indicate the turning point. You will be able to see a blue color with contrasting orange color pointing out areas of interest. The dots will indicate the entry points, exit points, collect profit points and so on. A stop point is also indicated just in case the trade does not work out as planned and you need to exit.

2. The Entry Zone Platform

We also have a swing trading platform known as the Entry Zone. This platform has been around for a while but has recently undergone a complete overhaul. It has received a new design to specifically address the needs of swing traders. There is no trader in the entire world who wants to join an over-extended market even when it features a large stop-loss point.

One of the main benefits of this specific platform is that it helps eliminate the challenge of entering an overly extended market. It starts by first checking for a pullback. It does this by accessing the 60-minute timeframe. This way, you will be protected from accessing the markets at the worst moment. The algorithm is able to proceed and track the markets so that you eventually get to find out the best market entry points.

3. Able Trend Trading Platform

This is another platform designed with swing traders in mind. One of its most outstanding features is its ability to instantly identify changes in the trend. Trend direction is first indicated by a distinct color. When the signal is headed upwards then the color is blue and when it heads downwards it changes color to red. If there is any sideways movement then the color changes once more to green.

This platform, therefore, makes it pretty easy to observe the market trend and keep abreast with it. Additional information will then enable you to make the necessary trade moves that you need to as a swing trader. For instance, you will notice red and blue dots on your screen. These indicate the various stop points. When there is a downward trend, then the red dots will indicate your sell points while blue dots will indicate your buy points on the upward trend. These stop points ensure that you partake of the large market movements but with very little risk or exposure.

The reasons why this system is so successful is that it comes with state of the art features. It generates dot and bar colors that you can choose for the different bar charts. These include the 5-minute, 1-minute, daily, tick, and weekly charts. Many traders have termed this platform as both robust and functional. It is a universal platform that can work with different trading systems.

You are able to make large profits if you are able to enter the markets and join the trend at an early stage. Identifying the trend is easy when you have this software. Remember that the trend is a friend of any swing trader. Therefore, spend some time at the beginning of your trades to identify the trend and then move on from here. Identifying the trend at an early stage is what you wish to do. The risks to you are minimal at this stage. This platform helps you identify the trend and provide you with additional crucial information that even large investors do not have.

You are able to operate on any market so that you are not limited to trading stocks only. If you wish to swing trade options, currencies, and other instruments, then you are free to do so. The platform is suitable for all trading styles including day trading, swing trading, and position trading, and so on.

4. Interactive Brokers

This is a popular platform that has been recently revamped. It is highly rated software because of the useful tools available to traders. Some of these tools are extremely useful to sophisticated or seasoned traders who need more than just the basics.

This platform is able to connect you to any and all exchanges across the world. For instance, you may want to trade markets in Hong Kong, Australia, and so on. The software is able to seamlessly connect you so that you have great trading experience.

This platform has seen the addition of new features which make trading even easier. These are, however, more suitable to seasoned traders who are more sophisticated than the average retail investor or small trader.

One of the attractive features of Interactive Brokers is that it is a very affordable platform to use. It is especially cost-friendly to small scale traders, retail investors, and the ordinary swing trader as the margin rates are low and affordable.

The platform supports trading across 120 markets located in at least 31 countries and deals in more than 23 different currencies. It also supports traders who execute trades pretty fast.

Trading and Data

As a trader, you will be making most of your decisions based on data. You, therefore, need to have access to reliable data such as stock prices and so on. Long term investors do not necessarily worry about accurate stock prices in the short term. However, for swing traders, it is essential to have access to the latest trading data.

The good news is that most online brokers provide traders with some form of data. All this data is mostly free. The platforms consistently receive data streams throughout. This data is crucial for most traders. Sometimes real-time data is not free and as a trader, you will need to determine which data you need and which type you will pay for. Always ensure that you have access to all the data you require during trading.

Chapter 4 The Channel Swing Trading Strategy

This swing trading strategy's one of the best ways to swing your way to profits. It's because apart from its cunning accuracy, it's also one of the easiest and most intuitive swing trading strategies you can use.

The really good news about most financial securities and markets is that they usually trade within a price band between 20% and 25%. This makes swing trading with this strategy easy to use with high potential for good profits.

The Price Channel Pattern

This particular pattern is created by two trend lines that are nearly parallel. The line above is the resistance line, while the one below is the support line. In a price channel pattern, price action's constrained within the two trend lines.

To take advantage of price channel patterns for swing trading, they need to be wide enough to provide potentially good swing trading profits. There are two ways you can use the price channel pattern for swing trading.

The first way is to buy at or near the channel's support line and sell at or near the resistance line. Pretty simple, huh?

The second way you can use the price channel pattern for swing trading profits is through price breakouts. These can create substantial price swings opposite the existing trend, which can provide excellent swing trading profit opportunities.

There are three general types of price channels: upward, downward, and sideways channels. An upward channel is one where succeeding highs and lows are higher. And consistent with channel patterns, prices move between the upward-sloping support and resistance lines connecting those increasing high and low prices. And when the price breaks out of these support or resistance lines, it's a trigger for taking or closing positions.

The Underlying Principle behind the Price Channel Swing Trading Strategy

You can minimize your swing trading losses if you clearly understand the market psychology underlying the Price Channel strategy. The primary reason why price channel breakouts can lead to significant price swings is due to the fact that a lot of traders trade within the channel. Most of them execute stop-loss orders above and below a price channel's resistance and support levels, respectively.

As the stop-loss orders accumulate outside a price channel pattern, smart money traders will eventually try and take advantage of these stop-loss orders. The reason for this is such massive stop-loss orders provide liquidity, which many smart money traders also need.

One thing you'll need to understand about price channel swing trading: all price channels are temporary, and price channel breakouts will eventually happen. The only question is: When will the breakouts happen?

Since most swing traders, especially beginners, aren't qualified to take short-selling positions, the assumption is that swing trading involves buying and selling of financial securities only. As such, we'll talk about the channels as follows:

The Price Channel Swing Trading Strategy –Selling

Step #1: Draw the Price Channel
First, draw a price channel when there's a minimum of two higher highs (HH) and higher lows (HL). Draw the resistance and support lines by simply connecting the higher highs and higher lows, respectively.

At this point, the goal is to identify distinct price actions that move within the channel, which are formed by the support and resistance lines you'll draw.

Step #2: Wait Until the Last Price Swing Fails to Hit the Upper Limit of the Price Channel

Particularly for an upward or bullish trending price channel pattern, a very telling sign that a price breakout from the channel's support line is imminent is when a security's most recent price swing fails to reach the upper limit of the channel, i.e., the resistance line. This indicates that the upward price momentum's beginning to lose steam and a trend reversal may be confirmed by an eventual falling through of prices below the channel's support line.

Keep in mind that the higher the number of times that an upward price swing fails to reach the channel's resistance or upper band, the higher the likelihood of a downward price breakout.

Step #3: Wait for the Downward Price Breakout to Happen and for a Confirmation

To minimize your risks for a false breakout signal or "whiplash," you'll need to do something else aside from wait for an actual price breakout to happen; wait for a confirmation signal for the said breakout. But what is a confirmation signal?

In particular, we're talking about Japanese candlesticks, particularly a Japanese candlestick breakout whose closing price is below the channel's support line. In short, don't just sell immediately as soon as a security's price falls below the channel's support line. Ideally, the Japanese breakout candlestick should look decisively big, though it isn't compulsory.

Step #4: Sell

Once you've confirmed the price channel breakout, it's time to sell your security at the Japanese candle's closing price.

It's that easy.

Setting Profit Targets with Fibonacci Retracement

This swing trading strategy can be used in conjunction with other swing trading strategies, including the Fibonacci retracement strategy.

For example, you can set your first profit-taking point at the 23.6% retracement level of the previous trend, the second profit-taking point at the 38.2%, and the third (should you choose to have one) at the 61.8% retracement level.

You may be wondering what the "previous" trend is. Well, it's the trend contained within the price channel pattern from which the price has broken out of.

Setting Stop Loss Orders

It's better to err on the side of caution, as the saying goes. While losses are inevitable at some point during your swing trading activities, you can minimize their amounts through automatic stop-loss orders.

As mentioned earlier, many swing traders set their stop-loss limits or orders outside of price channels, i.e., above the resistance lines or below the support lines. You can do this, too. But if you want to err on the side of caution, you might want to try and set your limits to above the last significant upward price swing.

Final Words

The Price Channel Swing Trading strategy can be used in any financial market trading activity, e.g., stocks, bonds, currencies, etc.

Keep in mind that one of the most telling signs of a potential price breakout or reversal is multiple failures to reach one of the channel's limits, i.e., upper or lower. When you see such failures, get ready to execute your swing trade.

Chapter 5 The Breakout Swing Trading Strategy

Breakout trading is a swing trading strategy that times trades when a security's price moves beyond an established price range for that security. Price ranges have upper and lower limits represented by resistance and support lines/levels, respectively.

Before discussing this swing trading strategy in greater details, it's important to know the two main kinds of breakouts: support and resistance breakouts and swing high and low breakouts. Let's talk about support and resistance breakouts first.

As you can probably glean from its name, these types of breakouts refer to incidents when a security's price moves significantly beyond a price range's established support and resistance levels. That's why it's important that you become very familiar with objectively drawing support and resistance lines, which was discussed in the support-resistance swing trading strategy.

When prices go out of an established price range or channel, is it already a breakout? When employing this swing trading strategy, you'll need to identify legitimate breakouts from fake ones. A legitimate breakout is one that's immediately followed by a large, bold Japanese candlestick, which closes significantly above or below a price range's resistance or support level, respectively. When it comes to breakout trading, the larger the Japanese breakout candlestick is, the better.

When prices break out of the upper limit, it's a good time to take long positions or close short ones. When the breakout of the lower limit, it's a good time to take short positions or close long ones.

Now, what about swing high and low breakouts? It works similar to the support and resistance breakout strategy, save for an extra filter. And that filter is set up to provide the highest chances for a profitable trade. You see, not all swing highs and swing lows are the same, i.e., some are better than others while some are worse than others.

For purposes of swing high and low breakout trading, we'll focus on one set up that works very well for many swing traders: the V-shape swing. A V-shape swing high is characterized by a very strong price climb that's immediately succeeded by a very strong sell-off, i.e., a substantial price drop. For price swing lows, a V-shape swing is characterized by a substantial price drop immediately followed by a strong price climb or rally.

It's tempting to want to believe that you can use breakout trading as your only swing trading strategy and profit happily ever after. Sorry to burst your bubble but that's a bad idea because breakout trading can produce a lot of whiplashes or false breakout signals. That's why you'll need to pair it with another technical indicator, one that you can use as a confirmation tool. What's this technical indicator?

It's the volume-weighted moving average or VWMA. As the last three words indicate, it's an exponential or weighted moving average, where each price entry has a different weight in the computation of the moving average. Unlike the EMA, however, the VWMA considers trading volume – not recency – as the basis for assigning weights to the price data components used in computing the average. While the EMA puts the heaviest weight on the most recent price and the least weight on the oldest one, the VWMA puts the heaviest weight on the price with the most trading volume and puts the least weight on the one with the lowest trading volume.

Now that you're aware of the need to use the VWMA for the breakout swing trading strategy, it's time to get right into the strategy.

Breakout Strategy for Taking Long Positions or Closing Short Ones

The first step is to identify either a V-shaped swing high. Once you do, mark that specific high price level as a resistance level, from which you'll draw a horizontal line. The point of doing this is to identify and recognize only those price levels that are both clear and significant.

The next step is to patiently wait until the security's price eventually breaks through that resistance level and its Japanese candlestick closes above that resistance level. That's the significant breakout you should wait for, which is a signal that the bullish traders have seized control from the bearish ones.

But wait...there's more! We need a final confirmation to really trust that the breakout is legit: the VWMA! When the VWMA confirms the breakout, that's your "buy" go signal! In particular, the breakout should happen with the security's VWMA stretching upward and leaning more towards a continued upside movement.

Once you've taken your position, place your stop-loss order for this trade at a price that's slightly below the breakout Japanese candlestick. Then, place your profit-taking order immediately or if you want to feel the market, when the security's price breaks below its VWMA.

A VWMA-oriented profit-taking strategy is based on the idea that when a price goes below the VWMA, it's highly likely that the rally-sustaining buyers may have already run out. The logic here is to lock in on profits before the security's price completely starts to rollover.

Breakout Strategy for Taking Long Positions or Closing Short Ones

The strategy here is the complete inverse of the one for taking long positions or closing short ones.

The first step is to identify either a V-shaped swing slow. Once you do, mark that specific low price level as a support level, from which you'll draw a horizontal line.

The next step is to patiently wait until the security's price eventually breaks below that resistance level and its Japanese candlestick closes below that support level. That's the significant breakout you should wait for, which is a signal that the bearish traders have seized control from the bulls.

When the VWMA confirms the breakout, that's your "sell" go signal! In particular, the breakout should happen with the security's VWMA plunging downward and leaning more towards a continued drop.

Final Words on the Breakout Swing Trading Strategy

One of the best things about using this strategy is that your trades are backed up by price momentum. This gives you a very good chance of executing more profitable trades than losing ones.

Another benefit to using this strategy is immediate feedback. You'll quickly learn if your breakout trading strategy will or will not work.

And lastly, consider the possibility of breakouts being driven by institutional investors' money. That may give a price breakout even more confirmation and support.

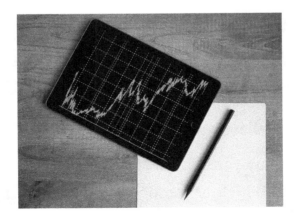

Chapter 6 Fundamental Analysis

Fundamental analysis is concerned with the well-being of the economy. The current progress of inflation, the interest rates, and balances of deficits among others is very important to fundamentalist analyst. They analyze the different political and economic situations of the countries to see the type of possible movements either short or long term the market is likely to make. Some of the factors fundamentalists consider are,

- **Interest rates**

The Federal Reserve's and the central banks look at the different economic indicators before they make the decisions on raising or lowering the interest rates in their respective countries. The rate of interest greatly influences the movements in the Forex markets. The higher the rate the lower the volume of trade and the vice versa is also true.

Averaging down incorrectly

Most people say that you shouldn't average down. The reality is that beginner trader should not average down. However, as you become more proficient or a lot better in trading, you become more successful in trading, there are certain situations that you may want to average down. This is because you put on a small tiny position and you prepared for a little bit of a pullback. When you have this experience, and you see a potential for the stock to continue to sell up a little bit, further that you don't mind buying it a little bit at a lower price because you're positioning for that situation and you are preparing for that situation in those cases and situations averaging down is perfectly fine. However, if you know you have the world in your hands and you are ready to go, and the stock is against you, and you start averaging down, and you start using the leverage, and you start putting more and more money to a losing trade that is automatically a wrong approach. This is not a healthy way that you want to average down into position. This is meant for gurus and money managers. Remembers nobody knows when the stock is going to go bankrupt. Be prepared that if you are averaging down, you can do it at most twice if you are new. But if you have experienced, you can work it out based on your strategies, maybe when the conditions are right, and you are prepared for them. You, therefore, need to catch yourself and save a position instead of losing it.

Using excessive leverage

You will always have this urge of trading more, especially if you are experiencing losing positions an. You were maybe trying to trade options, or you are using the margins because you don't have enough money. Most people do worse when they are using leverages. They don't understand how these things work. Therefore, they don't understand options, as options are more complicated, and you need to use more capital instances to make up those differences. You have to have the sock moving, especially if you are just buying puts or calls. Thus, at the beginning using leverage like options and margins, they become worse off than just buying three or five shares of a specific stock. Remember, if you don't have enough money, you are trying to use leverage or margin to make that difference. You need to start slow get better and build some consistency before you use the leverage. Use the too available to make more money instead.

Getting Emotionally tied to a stock

Often some traders get attached to a specific stock, and this is due to the emotional ties to a particular product or company. Maybe this is based on what you saw on twitter or social media platforms. You get emotionally tied perhaps because you use the product; thus, you are involved with the company. You have a relationship, and you, therefore, make investment decisions with no clear mind. If this is what you are also using when it comes to stock, ask yourself how it would be if the stocks turn around or selling off and you have no other plan in mind. You need to know that there have men many hundred successful companies that have failed over time. And you will realize that this is happening to many people. A lot of people put their money into specific equities, certain trading vehicles or believing in individual companies, and eventually, those stocks go lower and lower and lower and never come back up. You should, therefore, not get so emotionally tied to a particular stock. Don't be bothered by what the stock sells; however, all you need to care for is if the stock is moving. Is it continuing to make a certain consistent return time and time again? How is it behaving, how is the price action? Is it stable? To answer this, you need to look at your trading plan. Do not get attached if it is not; it is not talking or walking the right way to your plans. Be out of the trade if it is not doing something sensible to you.

Not taking profits into strengths

Most traders go into stock entirely and making the full profit once it reaches a specific number. You need to take profits slightly into depths as that stock continues running in your favor. This is because you never know when that blacks one day or date will come. You never really know when that stock will pullback. If an inventory is moving up, let us say two months you continue making higher highs, it is fantastic and enjoyable to you. Take a little money off the table. Take maybe a quarter, half, a fifth, or a third off into strength. Take that profit and put it back into your account and go ahead and do something elsewhere with it. Don't just allow the stock to continue to run higher and higher without taking any profit because the more the stretch, the longer that they keep stretching, the more likely it is going to have a pullback. Pullbacks are very healthy for stocks as they create new stock patterns, creates new opportunities and allows you to buy more shares from those profits that you took. The problem is that many traders when they have their issues, they get into a stock fully committed, and you don't make profits and allover sudden in one day the stock starts to go down even below your entry price. You need to note that the down days are much more violent, and one or two big down days can take one or two months' worth of gains. This is why it is crucial to take up money into strengths. You need not be scared of making up your profit. Yes, you do want your winners to run as long as possible, but you also need to know that not taking profits is just as bad as keeping it there.

Holding on to losers

The market will please some people and also annoy some people. I believe that you don't want to hold losers. Thus, you need not be tied emotionally to a particular stock. When you bought a stock at $50, it goes to $75, it now starts to sell up, and it then goes to $70 the $65 and then to $55 and gets back to 50 dollars that you bought it and you still hope that it goes up? If you continue holding just a little bit longer it will continue to go lower to $40 a share or $30 a share, you are now going to a fastener, and you are starting to lose money in a big big way. And now what people do is that they are at a loss and say that well am just so deep into it I might as well keep holding on to it. This is a big problem as you are holding on to losers longer than you should, especially if you had a profitable stock or a profitable trade. You should NEVER let a winning business turn into a losing trade that's why you take profits into strengths as mentioned earlier. Holding on to losers away too long is another huge mistake that you should avoid.

Chapter 7 Money Management

What Is Money Management?

This term is used to refer to the process of investing, spending, saving, and budgeting; it is also used to refer to the way capital is used for personal or group usage. The other words used for money management includes portfolio and investment management. When you are good with money, it involves a lot apart from just meeting your needs. When it comes to money management, having math skills is not mandatory, there are different skills needed that will be discussed later.

Money management is simply how you handle all the finances and how you handle all your long-term goals. It also involves how an individual manages their investment in order to make great profits. Most people think that great money management skills are all about saying no when you are tempted to make a purchase. What it really implies is when you are able to say yes to what is important to purchase. When you do not practice good money management skills, whatever money you have might look little for your lifestyle.

To have a good start when it comes to money management, you need to know where you are. This is in terms of your financial capability and power; like assets and liabilities. Assets include your investment and bank accounts, any properties and retirement accounts. Liabilities are the things that you need to pay like credit card balances, any loans like student loans and car loans and any mortgages and outstanding debts. Your net worth is when the value of your assets is more than your liabilities. And when your liabilities are more than your asset that is considered a net loss or negative net worth. When you have great money management skills and approaches, getting a net worth will be easy.

Ensure that you set your goals in order to achieve great money management. Your goals will create a plan on how you will manage your money. When you have your goals set, it will give clarity on which are priority expenses and which you can let go. You will need discipline and effort in order to achieve all your efforts. For instance, when you plan to buy a car worth $20k, you will need to work harder and smarter and reduce your expenses. You will need to do all that as compared to someone whose budget car is $10k.

When you have your budget drafted and set, remember to have adjustments. When you prepare a budget, you have the chance to know all the expenses that you have. For instance, you can set aside $150 that can be for entertainment and any miscellaneous expenses after payment of all expenses and managing your debts. Good advice is when you get a pay increment, do not use the additional income for your entertainment but add it into your savings.

When you have a target to meet different goals, you are likely to have the money in different multiple accounts. A good example will be to ensure that you have a separate emergency fund so as not to get tempted for any impulse buying in the future. You will also have different strategies and that will be for different goals. You will be aggressive when you start investing in different stocks that you will not need to invest money in like 20 years. You need to also have an account that has no risks like a savings account that that can be used as emergency funds when the need arises. When you have such multiple accounts, you can use a software program to help in tracking the several accounts. A good one can be Quicken; it will track all your expenses and the savings goals.

The Basics of Money Management

Money management is a term that deals with solutions and services that are in the investment field. The good thing is, in the financial market there are different resources available that can help in personal financial management. For any investor, their intention is to have a good net worth, so it will come a time when they will need the services of professionals like financial advisors. The advisors are known to offer brokerage services, money management plans, and private banking. The advice is best for retirement, estate planning and other benefits.

When you are in business, it seems complicated when there is a need to manage cash flow and different accounts. When you are able to strike a balance, you are guaranteed to be successful. If you are not able to manage all that, you will need to get the services of an accountant or bookkeeper to do all that for you. Even if you will outsource, you need to know the basics of money management and bookkeeping. You will need to know simple tasks like interpreting bank statements, understanding accounts payable and receivable, credit, and tax forms.

Money management will also involve knowing more about debit cards, checks, online payments, cash, and credit cards when it comes to payment options in your business. You will also need to have a planned and established payment plan and a debt collection system just in case of non-payment.

Opening a bank account is another way to help in money management, you need to choose a name and have an operating and registered business. Make sure you get more information on credit card facilities, a debit account, and any other additional services. Another important concept is to ensure that you have extended credit facilities in case of late payments. This can be planned for 30-6-90-120 days after a product is delivered or a service is rendered. You can motivate your customers to pay on time by extending discounts. Before the credit extension, ensure that you have done proper background check especially with large amounts. Even when there is credit extension, there are times where you will end up not being paid or not aid in time. To be able to recover your money, you need to ensure there is open and clear communication.

What Are Money Management Skills?

Before you can know of the best skills for money management, you will need to ask yourself some questions. What is your weekly or monthly income? Do you have a list of expenses that you need to pay? What you need to know is that money management is a skill used in life and cannot be taught in school. These skills cannot be learned in school but mostly from life experience.

✔ Have the ability to set a budget. This will help in tracking your expenses and the way you spend money. What do you spend a lot on, is it entertainment, clothes, or food? What is the tendency of overdrawing money from your bank account? If all that is yes, then you will need to set a budget. Look at your monthly statement and write down all the expenses in categories. You will be surprised by how much you are wasting.

✔ Spend what you have wisely. Always have a shopping list when you go shopping. Do you have a habit of looking at the product prices before putting it in the shopping basket? If you have coupons, ensure you use them. There are mobile apps and online resources that can help in focusing on your expenses. Do you know how to monitor your expenses? When you are not attentive to this advice, you will end up losing your hard-earned money.

✔ Always balance your books, do not always have a tendency of getting your bank balance online. When you depend on online information, there will be an issue when you want to know the balance on what you are spending at that particular moment. Be accountable and ensure you record all your expenses and this will help in avoiding any over-spending.

✔ Set a plan that will help in accomplishing anything that you put your mind. When you have a financial plan, you will be able to track how you are spending your money.

✔ Always think like an investor. When in school, you will not be taught how to handle money but largely on how to invest your money and have wealth growth. Learn to grow your savings and to invest at an early age. Turn that $100 to $200, $400, $800, and more. Having a stable financial future means that you have invested and grown in your money. When you start thinking like an investor, your money will grow. If you have a spouse or partner ensure that, they also know about your financial goals. If you possess a joint account with your partner or spouse, always work together and agree on the financial goals. When you are stuck or in doubt, consult a financial adviser and learn a lot of how to invest.

✔ Save your money, always be focused, and committed when it comes to saving money and this will guarantee a better future. This will help in improving your financial positiOn and even make it better. The first step is to have the decision to do that and this will help improve your management skills.

Importance of Money Management

Money management will help any individual in living on a budget and within their means. You will be able to look for great bargains and avoid any deals you believe that is not good when making a purchase. When you start getting a stable income, you will need to know how to invest because that will help in attaining your goals. And when you practice proper money management, you will meet all your goals and plans. There is the importance of money management:

✔ You will have better financial security: When you are careful with your expenses and savings, you will end up having enough for your future. Your savings will help in giving the proper financial security and you will be able to take care of yourself in case of emergencies. With your savings, you will not need to use your credit card in case of any issues.

✔ When you have proper money management and manage to save, you will be able to get opportunities and invest in the business. It will be frustrating to know of a great opportunity and not having enough funds to invest.

✔ Your credit scores will be determined by the way you manage your money. When you have high credit, score means you have managed to pay your bills on time and you have low-level debt. A high credit score means you will have more savings and you will be charged low interest when making purchases like cars or mortgages.

✔ Money management helps in reducing stress, this will happen when you start paying your bills on time. When you are late in paying your bills, you will encounter stress. Stress will bring about health problems like insomnia, migraines, and hypertension. You need to be aware of how you will handle money management, this will help in having extra cash and manage to save and manage a stress-free life.

✔ Money management helps in earning more money and when your income increases, you need to develop proper budgeting. And know of the right places to invest the extra money you have made. You need to know of additional venues to save money like in stocks and mutual funds; this will help in earning more money unlike money laying in your savings account. Ensure you learn about the investments, not all investments are profitable. The better thing about investments is that you can be on a monthly salary and still earning from your investment.

✔ When you adapt great money management skills, you will not waste money on unnecessary things. When you do not know how you are spending your income, it will be easy to be in debt. When you use your spare time effectively, it will help in managing your money. For instance, when you spend time with your friends and family members, ensure that you are aware of your budget.

✔ Peace of mind is guaranteed when you have better money management skills. When you a stable income and better savings, you will be able to handle any financial issues with confidence that all your needs can be handled perfectly.

World Top Money Managers

These managers are known to offer management and investment advice. They manage both active and passive funds.

✔ The Vanguard Group: It is a well-known management and investment firm, they have more than 20 million clients and in more than 100 countries. They started in Pennsylvania in the '70s and they have grown their assets to more than $5 trillion by close of 2018. They hold over 300 funds, move 150 in the US and more than 400 indexes to all of their market funds.

✔ Pacific Investment Management Company: This management firm has a worldwide presence and founded in California in the '70s. They have grown their asset base to more than $1 trillion by close of 2018. They have over 700 professional managing investments and with over 10 years as experts. They have over 100 funds and they lead in the fixed income sector.

✔ BlackRock, Inc: They started with their main company as BlackRock Group, by 1988 they started another division and labeled it BlackRock, Inc. They grew their assets to over $15 billion in 5 years and by the end of 2018, they grew to over $6 trillion and they have become the largest company in investment management in the world. They have over 100k in their workforce and over 50 offices in more than 30 countries. More than 20% of their assets are equivalent to $16 trillion.

✔ Fidelity Investments: This firm was founded in the '40s and by end of 2019 their customers have grown to over 20 million and more than $5 trillion in asset base. Their mutual fund is more than 300, this includes domestic and foreign equity, money market, fixed income, money markets and allocation of funds.

✔ Invesco Ltd: This firm has been in business since 1940 in offering investment advice. They announced in 2018, that they have made over $800 billion way above their products. They have over 100 EFTs that are made from their share capital. In 2017, they had a decline and it affected their stock price. They have managed to be among the best in the world despite all the challenges and setbacks. They have become among the top and best companies in the world, in terms of money, assets, and investment management.

The Approaches Used in Money Management

Great financial skills make money management easier, and how our money is spent largely affects your credit score and your debt cycle. There are tips that can help you if you are struggling with how to manage your money.

✔ Always have a Budget: Most people do not like to have a budget because they believe it is a boring and repetitive process. That involves listing all their expenses, summing up numbers, getting everything up, and running. When you have a budget, there is less room to be bad with money. You will get to know your income and expenses. The secret is focusing on the value that the budget will bring to your life instead of the budget creation process.

✔ After making the budget, the trick is to make sure that you use your budget. It will be a waste of time when you draft a budget and you do not stick to it. If it is a weekly or monthly budget, ensure that you refer to it often, and it will help when making your spending decisions. The budget should be made in a way that, at any given time you can easily track how much you have spent and know of any penning expenses.

✔   When drafting your budget, have a limit set for any unbudgeted expenses. In any budget, what is important to know is the funds left after paying all your expenses. When you have any budget and everything is settled, you can have the balance for your entertainment purposes. The amount set for fun should be a specific amount from your income. If you are planning to have a big purchase, refer to your budget first.

✔   Start by tracking your spending habits. When you have small purchases, they will end up piling and finally, you will notice that you have gone beyond your budget. When you track your spending plans. you will be able to know the places that you are failing and how you can rectify them. If you can, ensure that you save all your receipts and have a record of your spending in a journal. Have them in categories so that you can easily track them and know of the areas that are hard to stick on a budget.

✔   When your income is steady and qualifies you for a credit facility that does not mean that you should get that facility. You do not need to commit yourself to any monthly recurring bill. Most people think that the bank will not approve of the facility because they cannot afford it. What the bank knows is just your income exactly as you have reported. And if you have given a credit report, they will use what is offered on that report and they will not have any obligations not to give the credit facility. It is a personal decision to know if you qualify for the credit facility and if you have the capability to pay regarding your monthly income and other obligations.

✔ When making a purchase decision, ensure that you are paying the right and best prices. The best way to do this is by making a comparison and making sure that you are paying the lowest prices for the products and any services rendered. Look for discounts, cheaper alternatives, and coupons.

✔ In situations whereby you are planning to make a huge purchase, ensure that you save for that purchase. When you have the ability to delay gratification, will help in ensuring that you manage your money in a better way. It is advisable to out of large purchases, instead of sacrificing important things or tying a purchase to a credit card. This will help in evaluating if you really need the purchase or more time to do a price comparison. Ensure that you develop a habit of saving up instead of having a tendency to use credit cards; this will help in avoiding any interest on the cost price.

✔ Always limit the purchases that you do use your credit card. In situations whereby you run out of cash, chances are that you will end up using your credit card even if you cannot even afford the purchase and paying the balance. Learn to resist from using your credit cards when making any purchases that you know you cannot afford and especially on this that you do not need.

✔ Develop a habit of saving regularly. Open a savings account and ensure that you deposit money regularly; you can do it daily, weekly, or monthly depending on your income. This will definitely help in developing a healthier financial habit. Another better way will be to set up a plan that the funds are automatically credited to your account. That will help reduce the responsibility of reminding yourself to do that all the time.

✔ If you need to be a good manager when it comes to money, ensure that you practice it all the time. Plan when you intend to make a purchase and always buy what you can afford. When you make it a routine and a daily habit, it will be easier to manage money and the better for your finances.

Money Market Mistakes

To be successful in your investment in the money market, you need to ask yourself several questions/statements:

- Do you have an account for emergencies?
- The account that you have will be an investment
- That the funds you are setting aside will be useful soon.

When you decide to invest, you need to know that it is a risky venture and there are factors that you will need to consider first before any investment. For instance, when you decide to invest in a stock you need to know of factors like economic volatility. In the case of bonds, there are challenges like interest rates and inflationary risks. For a brave investor, leaning on a money market account will be a brave move. This is because they are known for safekeeping for the money. There are several mistakes when it comes to money market:

✔ The mistake that most investors make is thinking that money market accounts are the same as money market funds. They are financial instruments that have distinctive differences. Most people know of the money market fund as a mutual fund, the main characteristics are low returns and risks for every investment. They invest their funds in liquid assets for example cash. When invested in debt securities they have higher returns and ratings and mature in a shorter time. Most investors make the mistake and think that their money is safer in the money market, but that is not the same as with money market funds.

✔ Most people who are in investment believe that the money that they have in the money market is safe. The biggest mistake that they make is thinking that they are even safer from investments. Another belief is that, it better to have a lower interest rate with money in the bank than no interest at all. Most investors do not know the exposure they are in regarding inflation. This is the main reason that funds that are in the money market will not beat inflation. A good example is when the inflation rate is low than the interest that is claimed. Investors would know that, even though they believe the money market is safe, they are not safe from inflation.

✔ When in investment, you always need to know how to strike the right balance. Most of the time, the money market is influenced by inflation changes and rates. When you have such an investment, do not be tempted to input higher capital. They need a higher minimum balance as compared to the normal savings accounts. The normal account needs to be in operation for at least one year and have a higher amount of capital. When you have anything more than that, then it will be sitting their idle and it will lose value.

✔ Most investors like using money as their safety blanket. They believe that when they hold onto their money, it will be the best approach for any investment. This is not true especially when it is about savings whether in their money market or standard savings. It is not right to have your money exposed to uncertainty and any risk. This is one of the reasons why investors are afraid to invest and they would rather stay with their cash.

✔ To be a good investor, you need to know about asset diversification. When you are dealing with cash that is no different at all; this is because most people believe that cash is not an asset. You need to know that from the basics of finance and accounting, cash is known as a current asset. When you decide to hold on cash, ensure you do not hold more than $200k. It is not a coincidence to find any ordinary investor who has several bank accounts, in order to secure their cash. They have an approach to divide money or cash into three categories and that is a useful thing. The first one is to ensure that you have some money set aside for at least 3 years that is considered a shorter period. Around 4 to 10 years as the average timeframe and above 10 years as the longest timeframe. This is what will help the investors to know how long they can time their projects, how much is needed, and what will be saved in the end. This approach is important because it will also help in knowing about all the risks.

The best advice is to ensure that you invest in investments that are in the long-term and on lower risks. These will include investments like bonds, treasury bonds, life insurance, and annuity. You will need to know of the options that will help to avoid losing money value, avoiding any risks and the different ways about cash diversification. You can make use of the different trading and investment tools that will help in giving more returns instead of money market accounts. You need to look for investments that will help in creating more returns in a shorter time than the longer timeframe.

✔ Any investor needs to know that the reason for the money market is to hold money. When you have your money in just one place, you will not have any earnings or benefits; you need to move the money around. You will need to get more information on the different options and invest more. You should also know that money market accounts are not to be considered as long-term investments. The main reason is that they are subject to high interest rates than what is charged on a normal savings account. Hence not the reason to consider it a long-term investment.

✔ You should not be enticed to look for accounts that offer interest rates as a promotion. The reason is the interests are bound to change after some time.

Budgeting Apps

As an investor, you need to know that, with the tough economic times you need to know the best way to invest in the financial market. And when you become successful and start making money, you need to look for apps that will in managing your money. Thanks to technology all, those apps are easily available and easy to download. They can be downloaded and installed on tablets and smartphones; hence you can use them anytime and anywhere you are due to portability. The apps help is keeping you on track regarding the way you spend and how you spend.

✔   MINT:

Mint can be downloaded as an app or used as a website; it is in the budgeting and investment category. It is compatible with iOS, Web, Windows 8, and Android. It is more of a budgeting app and it will still help in managing your money. It has a feature whereby you can categorize and customize all your expenses and transactions. It has the ability to synchronize all your transactions from investments, bank accounts, and credit cards. They have a reminder feature for all your pending bills and this helps to avoid any lateness in bill payment that should be very convenient for any investor. All you need to do is set up a free account and then include all your financial details. This will then give a breakdown anytime an activity happens and you will be able to get a report.

✔   Good Budget:

This app uses the envelope concept, when you sign up you are given 10 free envelopes when you are on standard subscription. When you have an upgrade to Plus, you will then be charged a monthly charge of $6, and then you will have unlimited envelopes. The concept works in a way that, when your envelope is empty, you are not able to shop or spend any money. The other alternative is that you can move money among envelopes; this is because the app has the flexibility to use a common budget. You can share the budget with other people, the app is compatible with iPhone and all android devices.

✔ Dollar Bird:

This app also helps in money management; it manages future expenses and will remind you when you have payment dues. To set up and activate is free and it has additional premium features. Your budget will be broken down in a calendar form and your pending expenses will be visible. You have the chance to have all your transactions in categories that are color-coded and they will keep on adding up as you have repeated transactions. When you check on your utility bill and paycheck, they will be displayed there. You will be able to see all your current balance. What you can spend and still be on a budget. The main setback is that it does not synchronize will your bank accounts. The problem is you will need to manually enter all the transactions. The app is available for iOS users, Android, and the web. You will have the privilege to know about your income, expenses, and cash flow.

✔ EXPENSIFY:

This is considered an app and tool that is used to report expenses, track all receipts, and all the expenses that you have. The main advantage is that it helps in quick data entry and saves a lot of time doing data entry. You will have the opportunity to make all the entries in one click. This app is available for Android and iOS users, you will do all the capturing automatically and using OCR; this is a smart scan. All your reports are available by taking one picture and they are all uploaded and completed within a click. When you submit your expense, they get reimbursed faster and approvals are done very fast. When you use the app, you will be able to track all your expenses, categorize all of them, know the cost of all. All the expenses are consolidated and synchronized.

Chapter 8 Winning Entry And Exit Strategies

Monitoring Of The Main Order Types

Market orders

One thing to note about market orders is that they buy and sell at the current price, irrespective of what the price is. The market orders often get filled in an active market but not necessarily in the price the trader intended.

For instance, you may place a market order when the best price is 1.1954 but then other orders get filled first and your order might get filled at 1.1955 instead.

Note that market orders get used when you need yours to be processed but are willing to getting a slightly different price from what you wanted. If you are making a purchase, chances are that your market order will get filled at the asking price. This is mainly because that price is what someone else is willing to sell for.

On the other hand, if you are selling, there is a chance that your market order might get filled at the bid price. This is because that might just be the price someone else is willing to purchase at.

Entry And Exit Strategies For Part-Time Traders

There is a big difference between full-time and part-time trading. Part-time trading can be very tricky because trading does not always follow the usual trajectory.

One thing that is important to note is that trading is about quality and not quantity. In other words, if you do not get suitable trades, you can forgo trading those days even if it takes weeks at the same time.

However, just because trades are not suitable does not necessarily mean that you should not work. It is important that you keep educating yourself on how to interpret the watchlist and be ready for when opportunities present themselves.

Entering the fray

When you are trading part-time, your entry weapon is a limit order. However, if you have access to algo trading types, you can use an algo with an attached limit order. This means that, when a buy signal presents itself on a certain day, what you need to do is review how prices are behaving during the day so that you can determine the best point to place a reasonable buy order.

It is good to be choosy. However, if your limit order is not filled there is no big deal. Remember that there are plenty of fish in the sea and you only need to wait the next time to cast your net again. When you don't chase after the security so desperately, you can enter the trade on your terms soon as prices are favorable to you.

The last thing you want is trading the open market. It is chaotic when the emerging news after the market closed the day before is mirrored in the opening prices. Truth is, there can be major swings, both negative and positive.

The other point to note is to never enter a market order when the market is closed. This is because such a market order will be executed at the next day's opening prices, irrespective of what the price is. Truth is, movements are often fierce at the opening and entering market orders the previous day will be too much uncertainty of where the prices are likely to be executed.

What if you want to buy shares at the closing price the day before? The truth is that the market order will be executed here significantly above or below the price based on the prevailing conditions in the market. Just bear in mind the ol' Wall Street saying;

"Amateurs trade the open while professionals trade the close."

Exiting to cut losses or make a profit

When you buy stocks, the first thing that you need to do is set an initial stop loss point. This is important in ensuring that your capital is protected in case the stocks go against you. there are two major kinds that you can use in your exit strategy to cut losses or make profits. These are;

Physical stop loss order: This refers to an order to sell or buy (only if you are short) that you place with a broker

Mental stop: this simply refers to you clicking on the sell button or the buy button just so that you can exit the trade.

From a technical point of view, it really does not matter what type of stop loss order you choose to use. However, it is critical that before getting into any trade, you develop a plan that will help you determine when to exit the trade whenever things don't work out in your favor.

Are you a disciplined trader that always follows their plan through? If that's the case, then you are safe. This is because, when trading, it is always important to exit the trade based on your already predetermined plan. But where is that stop going to be?

Well, your stop should be sensible and out of the noise of current activities in sticks happening in the market.

But why use a stop clock? The truth is, when you buy stocks, you anticipate that they go in your favor. However, if things go south, you don't have to keep waiting for things to start moving in the desired direction. What you need to do is sell you shares and proceed to something else. The last thing you want is having all your capital tied up on a stock that is trading sideways. Treat your stocks like employees, if they are not performing, then fire them.

The second strategy is for you to use price alerts. If the prices cross at this level, you will want to be informed so that you can effectively manage your trades. The main aim here is to reduce the chart time so that you don't spend all your time doubting your original trade ideas.

With price alerts, you think way ahead on the level you would want to act. The what if scenarios will help you determine how you intend to manage your trades beforehand so that you can see where to exit and at what point your take profits will likely be. If you also want to scale in and out of positions, price alerts are a great option. All you have to do is set the alerts at suitable price levels and you are good to go!

Finally, you need to determine the right profit levels. According to statistics, it is safe to say that profit levels give better results if they are supported by market data. This simply means that for every trade, you need to know what the chart pattern, volatility data, and market structure looks like. This will help you know whether they support price movements in what direction.

Avoid setting take profit levels at random prices.

When you use this approach, you are better positioned to accomplish a number of things. First, considering that your take profits is not an arbitrary value, there is a high chance that the price moves to this level just to test it.

Second, it is important that you determine whether your Risk: Reward ratio is worth it depending on the levels that is directed by the data and structure of the market, which is more sensible.

So, how do I know my take profit level?

First, you need to look at the pair to trade and start looking for resistance and support on the chart. Look for regions of the chart where prices have seen bigger activities in the past. Well, this does not necessarily mean that prices will move to those levels. However, there is a tendency of prices retesting existing support and resistance levels as shown in the figure below;

In the case of a buy order, it is critical that you place your take profit levels a number of pips below the resistance. Conversely, when using a sell order, simply place the take profit level a number above the support. This accounts for everything like spread and is much safer than setting your stop loss on the actual level.

One thing you need to look for when determining the take profit levels is the trend lines, moving averages, and spikes in price activity. However, in my experience,

I have found that prices often adhere to horizontal levels.

Entry And Exit Strategies For Full-Time Traders

Benefit from intraday charting to time entry and exit

Did you know that day traders are traders that execute intraday strategies so that they can profit off of changes in prices for a set of assets? When you select the sweetest stock in the market, the next thing is for you to profit from them and the best thing is to rely on suitable strategies.

There are so many intraday strategies available in the market. However, sticking to the guidelines and identifying intraday trading signals can be challenging. So, when do you know when to benefit from intraday charting to time entry and exit?

Trade only with the current intraday trend

One thing you need to note is that the market often moves in waves. This means that it is the responsibility of the trader to ride the waves. When there is an uptrend, your aim should be to take long positions. On the other hand, if there is a downtrend, it is important that you aim at taking short positions.

The thing with intraday trends is that they do not continue indefinitely. When you have a dominant trend shift, then it is advisable to trade a new trend. But how can you isolate trends?

Well, this is the difficult part. With trendlines, you get an idea of where a useful entry and stop-loss strategy is. When you draw in more trendlines, you gain access to more signals that offer greater insight into the changes in the market dynamics.

Trade strong stocks in the uptrend and weak ones in the downtrend

If you are looking for stocks for intraday trading, the most beneficial thing is to look for ETFs or equities that possess at least a moderate to high correlation with the S&P 500 as well as the Nasdaq indices. After which, you isolate the stocks that are strong from those that are relatively weak based on the index.

This way, you create an opportunity for the day trader considering that strong stocks move up at least by 2% when the indices move a percent. Truth is, fast moving stocks offer more opportunity.

Reversion-to-the-mean trading

This is a theory that explains how extreme events are often followed by normal ones. In other words, there is a tendency for things to even out with time. For instance, you might see a soccer team score unusual goals in a match and in the coming matches, there is a chance that they will score closer to their average.

How do you apply this strategy?

The best way is to seek out extreme events and then bet that things revert to anything closer to the average. However, the only challenge is the fact that the financial market is not distributed normally. There is a long tail and there is a chance that extreme events cluster together. In turn, the feedback loops may escalate and create momentum which affects reversion.

When the stocks drop 10% on a certain day, chances are that they will drop even further the following day. Despite that, traders can use mean reversion to find an edge and then build their trading strategies around it.

When there is a simple mean reversion, you could buy stocks after a drastic drop in prices with the hope that the stocks will rebound to a normal level. There are so many ways in which mean reversion is applied;

- With technical indicators

- With Financial Information

- With Economic Indicators

- With Sentiment Indicators

Heikin-ashi technique

This is a technique that plays a central role in averaging price data with the aim of creating Japanese candlesticks that aim at filtering out all market noise. This technique uses a modified formula that is based on two-period averages based, which give the chart a smoother appearance. This makes it seamless to spot trends and reversals while obscuring gaps and price data.

What does Heikin-Ashi say? Well, this is often used by traders to identify a trend easily. When there is an uptrend, hollow white/green candles without lower shadows are evident on the chart. On the other hand, a downtrend is seen when there is a filled black/red candle without upper shadows.

Considering that the Heikin-Ashi technique smooths the price information over a span of two periods, it renders the trends, reversal points, and price patterns quite easy to spot. The thing with the Heikin-Ashi charts is that they typically have more consecutive colored candles that play an important role in helping traders identify past price movements with ease.

They also help in lowering occurrence of false trading signals especially in sideways and choppy markets, which helps one avoid placing trades at these times. For instance, instead of getting two false reversal candles before the beginning of a trend, using Heikin-Ashi technique increases the likelihood of getting a valid signal.

Limitations of the Heikin-Ashi technique

• Considering that this technique uses two periods, it often takes longer for it to develop making it quite unresponsive for day traders who would like to leverage fast movements in prices.

• The averaged data in this case also obscures important information on prices. In other words, the actual daily closing price is not seen on the Heikin-Ashi chart.

Back-testing

This is a general method used to see how well a strategy would have performed ex-post. The thing with back testing is that it assesses how viable a trading strategy is by simply uncovering how it is likely to play out with the use of historical data. In the event that back-testing works, this gives traders more confidence to apply it henceforth.

When optimizing your trading strategy, back testing would be the best way to go. When you simulate a trading strategy on the basis of historical data, you gain access to results that help you analyze risks and profitability before risking actual capital.

One thing you need to bear in mind is that if the back-test is conducted well and gives positive outcomes, then this is an assurance that your trading strategy is sound and has a chance of yielding profits when it is implemented. If the back-test is conducted well but the outcome is suboptimal, then there is a need to either alter or reject the strategy.

Key takeaways

- The market orders often get filled in an active market but not necessarily in the price the trader intended.

- Limit orders may or may not get filled and this depends on the manner in which the market is moving.

AVOID SETTING TAKE PROFIT LEVELS AT RANDOM PRICES.

- Traders use mean reversion to find an edge and then build their trading strategies around it.

- Averaged data obscures important information on prices because the actual daily closing price is not seen on the Heikin-Ashi chart.

- When optimizing your trading strategy, back testing would be the best way to go.

Chapter 9 Maintaining Swing Trading Momentum

One of the things you'll need to remember about swing trading momentum is that managing it well is more of a fine art than an exact science. To successfully manage your swing trading momentum, you'll need to learn how to manage your trading risks wisely, to be a very patient person, and master your emotions. Compared to day trading where all your positions are closed within a few trading hours, swing trading takes days, weeks, and even a couple of months to come full circle. Its longer time frame requires a different trading viewpoint.

The following are four important things you should do to maximize your swing trading momentum and consequently, profits.

Set and Forget

As mentioned earlier, you'll need a lot of patience to succeed at swing trading. You shouldn't be monitoring every price tick that happens all throughout the trading day. Once you take a long position, forget it. Just take a look at its price once a day or every other day. With swing trades, you'll need to let your chosen securities build their momentum so you can enjoy potentially high profits.

If you micro-monitor your swing trading positions, you'll put yourself in a position where you'll be strongly tempted to liquidate earlier than you need to. When you succumb to such temptations, you'll either minimize your trading profits or maximize your losses because you prematurely liquidated your position.

So, just set price alerts near your primary profit-taking and stop-loss target prices and forget it. Just take action when the alerts are triggered.

Ditch the Micro Time Frames

With swing trading, you must focus more on the longer time frames because they're less volatile and by doing so, you minimize your risks for "false triggers" or whiplashes that can make you take positions on securities whose prices are still on a decline. The shortest time frame you should consider is daily, nothing less. The longer your time frame, the lesser the false triggers and noise you'll encounter, and the more you can maintain your winning swing trading streak.

Moving Averages for Risk Management

The easiest and most objective way to see a security's true trend is through moving averages. As such, moving averages can be your best ally in managing your swing trading risks and find more profitable swing trading entry points.

Often times, financial securities that are enjoying momentum retreat to their moving averages, the most common of which are the 20 and 50-day moving averages, before proceeding with the next price movement. As such, moving averages can help you time your swing trades with fairly high accuracy and ease.

Don't Cash in on Your Profits in One Fell Swoop

Many financial securities that are on a strong price momentum can continue for weeks and months on end. But the challenge is it's impossible to predict exactly how long bullish momentums run for specific securities. There's always the risk of liquidating too early when a security's price continues to soar after closing a position and waiting too long that its price has fallen deep from its peak.

By taking partial profits or liquidating part of your swing trading positions on securities that are on a strong upward momentum, you can lock in on some of the profits once your chosen security has reached your target profit-taking level. Because there are still some left, you can lock in on more profits if the momentum continues. If the price happens to come down after that, your initial profits could compensate for the smaller profit or loss on the remaining position.

Money and risk involve in swing trading

At the point when utilized accurately, swing trading is a brilliant procedure utilized by numerous dealers crosswise over different markets. It isn't just utilized in the Forex advertise, yet it is an indispensable apparatus in prospects and value markets. Swing dealers take the abilities that they learn through specialized examination and can even parlay these aptitudes into different choices methodologies. The transient idea of swing trading separates it from that of the customary financial specialist. Financial specialists will in general have a more extended term time skyline and are not customarily influenced by momentary value changes. As usual, one must recall that swing trading is just a single system and ought to be used just when properly comprehended. Like any trading procedures, swing trading can be dangerous, and moderate methodology can transform into day trading techniques rapidly. In the event that you intend to utilize a swing trading technique, guarantee that you completely comprehend the dangers and build up a procedure that will probably enable you to produce greatest rate returns on your positions.

Distinguishing stocks and executing beneficial trading's

Every year, crowds of new dealers that don't have a clue how to make benefits trading on the financial trading come in huge numbers to take a stab at making a fast fortune yet end up regularly being significantly more unfortunate than when they initially started. In the event that you need to make exceptional yields and stay away from the shock of extensive misfortunes in the securities trading, at that point you should comprehend that specific basic achievement components are principal to elite in the trading the financial trading.

To start with, you should comprehend that value activity is the way to trading benefits. Value activity is the development of any security's cost and is outwardly spoken to on a value outline. The reason that it is indispensable to comprehend value activity is that cost uncovers where the patterns are so you can abuse them for benefit.

Regardless of whether cost goes up or down, bullish or bearish, your capacity to spot inclines in the financial trading is as to productive trading as water is to angle.

Without the capacity to comprehend value activity, you will always be unable to recognize client drifts and, are just, dead in the water.

Next, recall the old trading saying "the pattern is your companion" and stays with great with those patterns. Patterns can be your closest companion as long as you make sure to trading the course of a stock or security. Else, they can be your most noticeably terrible adversary, and it is nearly ensured that you will endure a long arrangement of awful misfortunes on the off chance that you trading against the force of the market.

Know your exit before your entrance is the following component that you should comprehend at a profound fundamental level in the event that you need to increase outsized benefits from the financial trading. In the motion picture, "Ronin," with Robert Deniro, Deniro plays a covert CIA specialist going into a bar late around evening time after it has shut to meet his contact. Prior to entering, he goes to the back of the bar, finds the secondary passage, puts a weapon by the exit, and after that strolls around the front and enters. Afterward, he clarifies that he never comes a structure without know where the entryway is and how to get out. This is solid ounsel for the secret covert agent as well as for the merchant too.

In the event that you're going to put a situation in any speculation, at that point you should realize when you will get out in case, you're regularly going to realize how to make benefits trading on the securities trading. This applies both to benefit taking and your leave methodology; on the off chance that a stock hits a benefit target, at that point take benefits with no of the psychological re-thinking or enthusiastic clashes of whether to sit back and watch on the off chance that it goes considerably further to support you or not (numerous brokers have transformed winning positions into losing positions by only overlooking their leave targets excessively long).

In like manner, if a position conflicts with you and you wind up assuming a misfortune, at that point you should not be reluctant to cut free that position since you're terrified of assuming a misfortune. Trading is based on little misfortunes while making immense benefits on out of control moves since you had the great sense to exit losing positions rapidly and ride the grand slam trading s to their fullest potential.

Figure out how to have an independent mind. You figure out how to think for yourself by placing in an opportunity to find out about value activity, how to adventure patterns for securities trading benefits, and realizing when to get out before you ever make a passage. Perhaps the main motivation for trading disappointment, if not the most critical reason, is that starting merchants come into the market without an arrangement or the preparation to fall back on in light of the fact that they do not have a comprehension of these center standards.

Recognizing Stock Market Pattern

A few people view financial trading as a way to procure income sans work. This isn't valid. Just individuals with a touch of good karma could have benefits in the event that it was that simple. Individuals engaged with trading stock have done some examination to make a benefit. Recognizing the patterns of the market is the way to achievement in the financial trading. In the event that you can distinguish the patterns in financial trading, you can comprehend the conduct of a stock dependent on its past exhibition.

One of the fundamental presumptions of stock promoting organizations is that the market has patterns: essential, optional (present moment) and mainstream patterns (long-term). In view of these patterns, showcase watchers foresee the estimation of offers. Merchants use examples to recognize benefit or misfortune.

The securities trading can be a positively trending business sector or a bear showcase. A positively trending business sector shows the nearness of a larger number of purchasers than venders. This prompts an expansion in the estimation of offers. Despite what might be expected, if the quantity of venders is more than the quantity of purchasers, the measure of offers falls. It is said to be a bear showcase.

To distinguish a pattern, you need data on two basic elements of the financial trading: cost and volume. The value informs you concerning the course of development in the market, and the sum says whether there is development in the securities trading. There are situations when the volume of a stock is high, as is its cost. This demonstrates an upward pattern. On account of high limit and minimal effort, it is a descending pattern. In view of this, you may choose whether to sell or buy stocks.

In the event that you see customary descending days, the market is showing a slow down or upswing. It is astute to put resources into stocks as costs will undoubtedly hop back. On the other hand, in the event that it has been a nonstop time of high rates, the market is showing lower costs later on. It is the correct time to exit from the stock.

Frequently, it happens that the stock costs are expanding or diminishing. This may resemble a change to you. In any case, in the event that you look at the volume and find that there is definitely not a significant volume increment or lessening, you ought not anticipate a distinction in the securities tradingyet. While contemplating patterns is a decent propensity in securities trading, it is important to watch out for false flag.

Stocks, which are high in volume, for instance, common assets, will in general influence the development of the market. You can watch out for activity in such stocks to recognize potential changes. A few internet trading organizations give outlines and pattern pointers on their sites. These apparatuses can be utilized to consider the patterns in financial trading.

Before we dig into distinguishing stock patterns, allows first characterize what a pattern is "a predominant propensity or tendency" or "a line of general bearing or development." "pattern" is likewise utilized as an action word and signifies "to grow a general way." The utilization of the word pattern about the financial tradingwould then imply that a stock that is inclining is a stock that is moving a general way.

Stocks just move in three distinct ways, they climb, they go down, or they move sideways. Stock patterns are regularly discussed as far as either a bullish pattern, which means the stock cost is expanding or a bearish pattern, which means the stock cost is diminishing. On the off chance that a stock's cost is essentially going neither up nor down, yet moving sideways, it may not be seen by some to be in a pattern. In fact, for example, stock is a sideways way. The sideways example is additionally generally alluded to as a "time of combination."

There is any number of approaches to distinguish stock patterns. Probably the most straightforward approaches to do this is to take a gander at a stock graph. Stock diagrams are pervasive and can be discovered everywhere throughout the Internet at such puts as Yahoo Finance or Google money. In case you're taking a gander at a stock outline and the latest cost is higher than the past rates the stock can be said to be in an upswing. On the other hand, in case you're taking a gander at a stock graph and the latest costs are lower than the past costs on the table then the stock is said to be in a downtrend.

We have quite recently perceived that it is so natural to distinguish stock patterns. There is a significant inquiry that is on the psyche of everybody hoping to recognize a pattern. That question is, "does this pattern have the solidarity to proceed?" You see, when you distinguish an example, it simply isn't sufficient to know which course the market has been going, however which heading the market is well on the way to go from here. This is the reason it is basic to decide the quality of any pattern. The explanation behind this is. In a perfect world, we would get in on a pattern that has great force, the kind of vitality that could convey the stock cost toward a path that will make us a brilliant benefit.

There a few different ways to quantify a pattern's quality or shortcoming. Numerous investigators depend on the trading volume as a pointer that the intensity of the example is either expanding, diminishing, or staying generally the equivalent.

So, when you are thinking about your next stock trading doesn't just mull over what the pattern has been, however more significantly, if that pattern is probably going to proceed.

Distinguishing the Right Stock Market Trading System

Fruitful trading relies upon three factors: the dealer's brain science, the capacity to oversee cash, and a financial trading framework that is exceptionally viable. This article talks about the securities trading framework and how brokers, particularly the apprentices, can decide on a framework that is appropriate for his trading style.

Simply ask the expert brokers who have turned out to be fruitful in this field throughout the years. They have a trading framework that produces winning stocks. They won't be the place they are currently if their financial trading framework does not work for them.

No two dealers are similar. In this manner a trading arrangement of one doesn't really imply that it will work a similar route for another. A few brokers put resources into their qualities while others deal with their shortcomings. A few frameworks plan to buy the estimation of the stock in the long haul. Others focus on the transient expense. The trading framework relies upon the brain research of the merchant too.

There are approaches to benefit from the financial trading framework, however there is one component that a dealer must need to succeed. They must be methodical. This implies the trading framework that works for them ought to be something they stay with all through their trading vocation, regardless of what occurs. The financial trading framework develops however the methodologies that they detailed dependent on the experience and the exercises that they gained from the mix-ups they unintentionally made can be their mystery to pick up the speculations they have as a primary concern. To put it plainly, merchants choose dependent on their methodologies and not their feelings.

Another mystery is to thought of a framework that fits the dealer's character. It resembles a couple of pants. It's difficult to look for the correct pair of pants on the grounds that the fit is fundamental. It resembles the securities trading framework for dealers. They should create one that they are alright with and can give them the outcomes that they need, in light of how they see themselves in their trading vocation.

Along these lines, the securities trading framework must be from a system which expands the qualities and limits the shortcomings of brokers. The present circumstance of the market should likewise be considered. Once in a while, dealers need capital development or income with the goal that their salary from trading can be made into benefits they can live on. On the off chance that dealers are certain about their aptitudes and have enough money to contribute, at that point they can continue with ongoing trading.

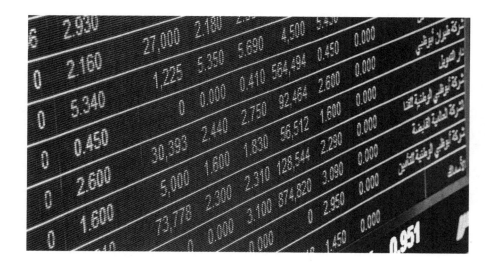

Chapter 10 Improving Swing-Trading Methods And Reducing Risks Involved

There are several swing trading methods used by traders. Despite their effectiveness, something can be done to improve them. Traders face a myriad of risks because of swing trading strategies that do not work as expected. The best way to help traders avoid making losses every day is to find problem areas and deal with them. The first way to improve swing-trading methods and reduce risks involved to ask swing traders what they want to be done. It is not right to assume that we know challenges faced by swing traders. They are the ones who trade using the strategy and their input is vital. There is a saying that goes "only the wearer of the shoes knows where it hurts or fits" and that applies in this case. You do not have to ask every swing trade to comment on the strategy as that will be cumbersome. You only need to involve a few beginners and long-term ones. Once you hear their suggestions, seek ways to implement them. For example, if swing traders say that a certain aspect makes trading difficult, list it and determine how to improve it. One of the reasons why traders end up leaving companies they started with is because of neglect. Some firms do not care whether swing traders are having a rough time using their systems. They are only concerned about increasing the number of traders. This is an attitude that companies need to change if they want to last long in the business. There are many trading companies that have emerged which means that traders have options. You cannot provide shoddy services and expect customers' loyalty. Instead, create an open communication platform where traders can talk freely and discuss issues they are facing. Doing this will not only improve trading but also increase the number of traders.

Another way to improve swing-trading methods and minimize risks is to use a strategy that works for you. If you are kind of person who does not like to be glued on the screens, do not opt for a strategy that requires you to do that. Trading experts advise you to take time before you choose a strategy. There is no point of rushing things and end up with regrets. Moreover, do not pick a strategy because it worked for someone else. This is a big mistake that many make in the trading markets. Your friend could have chosen a certain strategy because he has someone helping him or is just good at trading. When you get into trading because of someone else, your chances of lasting long in the markets is limited. You lack the drive to continue in the midst of challenges. Soon you realize that you made a mistake and want a way out. Choosing a strategy that fits your lifestyle increase chances of success. It also makes swing trading easy and worthwhile.

Another way to improve swing-trading methods and reduce risks is to have a mentor. No one was born knowing everything and we need each other. While it is true that not everyone means well, you cannot miss finding even one who is willing to help. This is extremely important for beginners who are green in the markets. You can monitor the stocks and charts but that does not compare to one on one you receive from an experienced person. If you are having trouble finding someone to mentor and help you pick the right strategy, consult a professional. You will spend extra but it will help you avoid making mistakes. As a beginner, you must be willing to try different strategies to seek which one works. Do not make a huge investment at first because you are still surveying the markets. You cannot put all your hope in a single strategy. Some traders stick to one swing trading strategy despite suffering losses. They do not see the need of trying other options because they do not want to risk. One thing you need to know is that making a loss in the markets is unavoidable. Even the best swing trading strategy fails sometimes. You just need to make wise investment decisions and be willing to accept the outcome.

Another way to improve swing-trading methods and reduce risks involved is to study courses offered on chosen strategies. There are several training courses online you can take to sharpen your skills in a given strategy. Do not make the mistake of assuming that you know everything. This will be your downfall, as you will not see when you go wrong. There is a reason why those training courses are offered in the first place. Some are free and others you pay a small fee. Do not be rigid and afraid to spend more. If you do not spend money to get ready before you start trading, you will lose it all in the markets. Trading strategies have flaws that can be improved just like your mindset and attitude towards swing trading. If you only work to improve the strategies and forget your personal input then you are cheating yourself. A swing trading strategy is effective when a trader knows what he is doing and is not afraid to take risks. At the end of the day, you are the one who determines whether the chosen swing trading strategy works or not. Pick what works for you and survey the rest. Just because you have chosen, one strategy does not mean that you cannot consider or use others. A swing trader must be flexible to tap into the markets. This also applies to the trading strategy you choose. Be someone who moves on quickly when one strategy fails.

You can also improve swing-trading strategies and reduce risks involved through careful planning. A plan is essential even in the corporate world. You cannot start a business or build a house without a plan. Similarly, a swing trading strategy needs careful planning. In some cases, traders are responsible for the failure of a trading strategy. They do not plan how to use different methods and whether they have the necessary skills. Before you jump at something, drawback and understand how it works. Having a plan minimizes risks because you know how to mitigate them. Moreover, you can foresee risks and act before they become worse. As a swing trade, know different trading strategies in the market and organize yourself.

Improve swing-trading strategies by learning from experienced companies. New firms should take time to understand how the industry works before starting operations. It is not bad to look at how others are doing things. It is only bad when you copy everything they do.

Before using a particular swing trading strategy, find out as much as you can about it. What are the benefits of using the strategy? What are the risks? What can I do to make it work for me? These questions will enable you to find areas you need to work on and make the right decisions. At the end of the day, do not be stuck with a swing trading strategy that is not working. If you have tried everything but it is not working, choose another strategy. This time, take time to analyze a strategy before using it. One of the reasons why swing-trading strategies do not work is because we put high leverages and blame the failure of the strategy. There is no way a strategy can work if you do not buy the right stocks and make good decisions. Everything boils down to what are you doing to make it work.

You can make a strategy work by using tools and indicators. There is a reason why tools and indicators are part of trading. You should analyze charts, and use various tools to trade smoothly. People who implement several tools in a trading report a few cases of failure, compared to those who do not use any of them. We have established that we hold the key to success or failure in the markets. A trading strategy will not work if you are the kind of person who is controlled by different emotions. If you cannot separate your emotions from trading, it is better to exit the markets. There will be days when you feel like giving up because of losing everything, but if you remain firm and use the right strategy, you may gain more than you lost.

Conclusion

Thank you for buying this book. I hope that through it, you were able to understand what Swing Trading is all about and more importantly, how to do it.

But knowing is only half the battle. The other half is action or application of knowledge. To make the most of what you learned and make it impact your life, you must apply the things you learned about swing trading in this book. Otherwise, everything you've read here is just for entertainment.

You don't have to apply everything at once. Start with one or two lessons for the next few days. Then apply another one or two for another few days and so on until you're able to apply what you learned and profit from swing trading.

So, what are you waiting for? Here's to your Swing Trading success my friend! Cheers!

CPSIA information can be obtained
at www.ICGtesting.com
Printed in the USA
BVHW041450020321
601493BV00011B/978